Bretton Woods revisited : evaluations
of the International Monetary Fund
and the International Bank for
Reconstruction and Development /
papers delivered at a conference at
Queen's University, Kingston, Canada,
and edited by A.L.K. Acheson, J.F.
Chant, M.F.J. Prachowny. -- Toronto ;
Buffalo : University of Toronto
Press, c1972.
xxiv, 138 p.
Includes bibliographical references.
Photocopy. Ann Arbor, Mich. :
University Microfilms International,
1981.

Bretton Woods revisited : ... c1972.
                                      (Card 2)

1. International finance--Congresses.
2. International Monetary Fund.
3. World Bank. I. Acheson, A. L.
Keith. II. Chant, John F.
III. Prachowny, Martin F. J.

BRETTON WOODS REVISITED

Bretton Woods Revisited

EVALUATIONS OF THE
INTERNATIONAL MONETARY FUND
AND THE INTERNATIONAL BANK FOR
RECONSTRUCTION AND DEVELOPMENT

Papers delivered at a conference at
Queen's University, Kingston, Canada
and edited by
A.L.K. ACHESON
J.F. CHANT
M.F.J. PRACHOWNY

UNIVERSITY OF TORONTO PRESS

© University of Toronto Press 1972
Toronto and Buffalo
Printed in Canada
ISBN 0-8020-1847-5
Microfiche ISBN 0-8020-0175-0
LC 72-185697

To our wives
Mary, Bev, and Marguerite

Contents

Preface

On 2nd and 3rd June 1969 a conference was held at Queen's University to commemorate the twenty-fifth anniversary of the Bretton Woods Agreements. The purpose of the conference was to assemble a number of scholars who share an interest in the workings of the present international monetary arrangements, their antecedents, and their development in the future. The purpose of publishing the proceedings of the conference is to share these thoughts with a wider audience.

In arranging the conference and preparing the manuscript for publication, the editors received valuable assistance from a number of sources. Financial support for the conference, which was provided by the Canada Council, the Canadian Bankers Association, and the Institute for Economic Research of Queen's University, is gratefully acknowledged. In addition, this book has been published with the help of a grant from the Social Science Research Council of Canada using funds provided by the Canada Council. These institutions are not necessarily in accord with the views expressed at the conference. Our colleagues, particularly David Smith, were constant sources of encouragement. Mrs Heather Werry performed housekeeping functions with cheer and competence. Finally, and most importantly, the editors would like to thank the authors, discussants, and other contributors for their efforts in making the conference a success.

Kingston, Ontario

A.L.K. Acheson
J.F. Chant
M.F.J. Prachowny

Introduction

On 1 July 1944 the United Nations Monetary and Financial Conference began its deliberations at the Mount Washington Hotel in Bretton Woods, New Hampshire. It was to be the most important conference on international financial arrangements since the London Conference of 1933. The meetings at Atlantic City which just preceded Bretton Woods were preliminary discussions; the Savannah Conference of March 1946, which represented the inaugural meeting of the International Monetary Fund, dealt mostly with minor points of contention. Thus it was at Bretton Woods that in twenty-two days the delegates of forty-four countries, plus observers and technicians totalling 730 persons, drew up the main documents which they hoped would shape international economic relations in the postwar period.

But the problems faced at the Bretton Woods Conference over a quarter of a century ago are not the problems of today. In the intervening years we have witnessed major changes in international adjustment policies and a growing awareness of the need to transfer resources from rich to poor nations. While the main economic problems facing policy-makers in 1944 were reconstruction of the war-ravaged areas of Europe and elimination of the debilitating effects of North American balance-of-payments surpluses and European deficits, the focus has shifted to providing equitable and efficient aid to underdeveloped countries and to rectifying the weaknesses of the key-currency system. A question that naturally arises is whether the two institutions founded at Bretton Woods, the International Monetary Fund (IMF) and the International Bank for Reconstruction and Development (IBRD), were designed with sufficient flexibility to accommodate these changing needs or whether they were rigidly cast in a mould suitable for 1944 but outdated by 1969. It therefore seemed appropriate and desirable to analyse the present and future usefulness and resourcefulness of these institutions. A conference at Queen's University on 2 and 3 June 1969 was held in order to provide a forum for such an analysis, and elaborated versions of the papers presented there provide the material for this volume.

In this introduction we hope to set the papers of the volume in perspective and to highlight the important issues. No attempt is made to compete with Professor Harry Johnson's discussion which appears as the final paper. Johnson provides an overview of the varied fare presented at the Queen's conference. As any reader of his work has come to expect, Johnson brings unusual insight to his task, at times relating apparently diverse points, at others assessing critically speakers' contributions, and often elaborating their implications. Still, Johnson focuses his attention mainly on selective analytical issues. To supplement his comments we have provided a brief summary of the main issues raised by the participants. In particular this summary emphasizes points where the authors' interpretations are likely to be controversial. Many of them examined the significance of recent changes in the international financial system and to assist the reader we have outlined the features of several of these changes.

Since the time of the Queen's conference the international financial system has continued in a state of flux, the most dramatic uncertainties lasting from President Nixon's declaration of the inconvertibility of the dollar in August 1971 to the Smithsonian Agreements of 17-18 December of the same year. This summary describes briefly the issues involved in the crisis and the final agreement. In addition, interrelationships are developed where the events of the last half of 1971 bear heavily on themes running through this volume.

Two aspects of the Bretton Woods meetings received particular attention at the Queen's conference. First, the views of the participants at Bretton Woods were examined in terms of their expectations of the difficulties facing the international financial system in the postwar world. Second, explicit attention was directed to the political and economic forces that shaped the reconciliation of the British and American plans for the reform of the international monetary system. For consideration of the present and future, the conference format followed the division of responsibilities between the two Bretton Woods institutions: the International Monetary Fund and the International Bank for Reconstruction and Development. The achievements of each institution were evaluated by considering their successes and failures in relation both to the problems initially expected and the unforeseen problems that subsequently arose. Finally, the institutions were judged in terms of their ability to face the problems of an uncertain future, tentative though such judgment has to be.

An awareness of the atmosphere shaping the thinking of the delegates to Bretton Woods is essential to an understanding of the achievements of the meetings. At the time, the participating countries were still engaged in the war, with several represented by governments-in-exile. The memory of the depression with its international financial chaos was also firm in the delegates' minds. Bretton Woods was therefore seen as an opportunity to exploit the co-operative spirit among the allies for the purpose of creating a superior economic order for the postwar years.

The Bretton Woods agreements were only part of a broader movement toward international co-operation. The IMF and IBRD were seen by many as an element in a complex of postwar arrangements for international economic co-operation. The IMF was to be responsible for international payments; the IBRD for the transfer of resources to reconstructing and developing economies. Moreover, there was to have been the International Trade Organization (ITO) concerned with commercial policy. Unlike the others, the ITO failed to gain ratification from its member countries and did not come into existence. In its place remained the more limited General Agreement on Tariffs and Trade (GATT), originally intended as a temporary expedient.

To analyse the interplay between the economic and political forces at Bretton Woods, Sir Roy Harrod, biographer of Lord Keynes, was invited to present a paper on the postwar problems of the international financial system as perceived by the participants at Bretton Woods. Sir Roy, though not directly involved in the negotiations leading to Bretton Woods, was in an exceptional position as a confidant, subject to the Official Secrets Act, to observe the development of Keynes' thought and the forces influencing it. Sir Roy recalls the postwar negotiations as involving a trade-off between American interest in commercial policy and British interest in international monetary arrangements. In their initial position papers the Americans expressed the hope that many of the restrictions imposed on international trade and payments during the depression could be dismantled, while the British wanted to maintain the system of imperial preference and the sterling area. At the same time the Keynes plan, representing the British viewpoint, envisaged the IMF as a quasi-automatic source of financing deficits in the balance of payments, while the White plan, offered by the Americans, saw a more limited role for the IMF. In addition, while the British argued for little or no political interference with the international organizations established at Bretton Woods, the position of the United States was that political considerations could not always be subservient to economic factors.

In the final section of his essay Sir Roy calls attention to a number of areas where he feels the workings of the present arrangements do not correspond with the ideologies of their founders. From a theoretical standpoint Sir Roy questions the contemporary application of Keynes' doctrines to current conditions of price inflation. While 'Keynesians' today advocate restrictive measures to reduce excess demand, Harrod feels Keynes would likely reject this interpretation of his theory. As a challenge to the 'conventional wisdom' Sir Roy asserts three propositions:

1 raising taxes, whether direct or indirect, is inflationary;
2 high interest rates are inflationary;
3 damping demand is inflationary, except possibly in a very short period.

Insisting that economic theory has nothing against these propositions, Sir Roy argues their validity can be verified or falsified only by examination of empirical evidence. Acceptance of these propositions would overturn most of the economists' prescriptions for limiting inflation, with consequences similar to those of Keynes' *General Theory*. Sir Roy, however, does not spell out the policy measures for halting inflation implied by his theory.

Present approaches to the problems of developing countries are judged by Sir Roy as unlikely to be adequate to meet future needs. Among the alternatives which he views favourably are the Stamp plan for issue of gold notes to be channelled through the IBRD, use of buffer stocks to sustain prices of primary products, and long-term commitments by developed countries to purchase manufactured products of the developing countries.[1] To many economists and others, his proposals will appear to conflict with the principles and rules of existing agencies. Sir Roy, however, maintains that a rethinking

1 The essential feature of the Stamp plan was the attempt to integrate international reserves with development finance. Underdeveloped countries would receive the gold notes with which they could purchase goods and services from the industrial countries, who would then acquire the notes and use them in settling deficits in their balance of payments. The interested reader will find further discussion in H.G. Johnson, *Economic Policies toward Less Developed Countries* (New York 1967), p. 266. Further reading on buffer stocks is contained in Chapter 7 of the same book, while the proposal for developed countries to open markets for manufactured goods from underdeveloped countries is discussed in Chapter 6.

along the suggested lines would not be displeasing to some of the architects of the present arrangements who regarded their work as only a beginning.

Professor Richard Gardner sets out the relative roles of political and economic factors in shaping the final choice at Bretton Woods, with particular emphasis on the American point of view. While not a participant at Bretton Woods, Gardner, author of *Sterling-Dollar Diplomacy*, ranks as one of the outstanding experts on the negotiations at Bretton Woods and their antecedents. In his paper he suggests the ironic consequences of the division of responsibilities in Roosevelt's cabinet and of the relations between Roosevelt and members of his cabinet. Roosevelt apparently had a close personal relationship with Henry Morgenthau, his secretary of the Treasury and a Dutchess County neighbour. However, Roosevelt was not as close to Cordell Hull, his secretary of state responsible for trade negotiations. The primacy given to the financial side of postwar planning is partly explained by the relationship between Roosevelt and Morgenthau. With a different division of responsibility for commercial and financial policy there might have been the ITO, and not the IMF. The effects of this division of responsibilities between the Treasury and the State Department persist today in the anomaly that when a country has balance-of-payments problems its use of trade restrictions is discussed by GATT whereas its need for financial aid or its use of exchange controls is discussed by the IMF. Heeding the example of the ITO and its rejection by the United States Senate, Gardner stresses that proposals acceptable to Congress were needed to assure the creation of the IMF and IBRD. As a result, Gardner admonishes those critics who would judge the Bretton Woods institutions purely from an economic perspective.

As one of the participants observes, the Bretton Woods Conference was very much 'an ABC affair: America, Britain, and Canada'. The disproportionate importance of Canada was the result of the wartime disorder in many countries and the fact that three major countries, Germany, Italy, and Japan, were still regarded as enemies. A unique and important feature of the Conference at Queen's was a roundtable discussion involving four Canadians who were delegates at Bretton Woods and who have participated actively in shaping postwar economic policy in Canada: Louis Rasminsky, W.A. Mackintosh, A.W.F. Plumptre, and J.J. Deutsch. The participants in the round table were not given any explicit instructions, but were invited to make observations on any aspects of the Bretton Woods agreements. Consequently, the summary of the roundtable discussion provides the reader with several different perspectives on the Bretton Woods Conference.

It is interesting to note that most of the speakers who were participants, directly or indirectly, at Bretton Woods were almost totally sympathetic to the outcome of the Bretton Woods arrangements, dismissing faults as unforeseen problems or minor vexations. No one took the radical stand that Bretton Woods was irrevelant or a hindrance to a more smoothly operating international monetary system and to a more equitable and efficient method of transferring resources to underdeveloped nations. The one area which received some criticism by Gardner, Rasminsky, and Plumptre was the system of choosing IMF executive directors. While they favoured highly-placed part-time directors, the IMF in fact has full-time directors drawn from the middle level of the civil service. But this attack on the format rather than the substance of the Bretton Woods arrangements points out the overall sense of achievement displayed by the founding fathers: the mere existence of the IMF and IBRD was sufficient proof of triumph.

Between the Fund's early years and the present the international monetary system had changed considerably. With the achievement of current account convertibility for the main European currencies in 1958 and a subsequent easing of controls over capital flows, the probability of more violent fluctuations of balance-of-payments positions increased. In order to ensure that it would participate in the financing of stabilization programmes initiated by deficit countries, the Fund made increasing use of stand-by credit arrangements. Under these arrangements members receive lines of credit if the Fund approves of their stabilization programmes. The existence of such negotiated potential credit may persuade speculators that the government of the country whose currency is under attack has the means to carry out its proposed policies. Such a show of strength may curb hot money flows which could force an unwanted and unnecessary devaluation.

The Fund was also concerned that the increased call on its resources would deplete its holdings of currencies that were acceptable to borrowers. In 1961 an agreement was successfully negotiated with the major countries to lend their currencies to the Fund if it was necessary 'to forestall and cope with an impairment of the international monetary system.' Despite these responses by the Fund, bilateral arrangements between major central banks have provided an increasing share of the conditional credit available to an industrial country incurring balance-of-payments difficulties.

The leading industrial economies have found that it is beneficial to co-ordinate balance-of-payments policies under a system that frowns upon parity changes. The IMF has provided a forum for discussions of policy problems, but the most effective co-operation has been forged at meetings outside the IMF umbrella between officials of the financially important countries.

The increase in conditional credit available to deficit countries and the greater co-operation among central banks represent gradual responses of the international system. The agreement on deliberate creation of reserves and the development of a two-tier gold system were more dramatic and abrupt reforms. These recent innovations were ever-present influences on the discussion of the evolution of the IMF.

The IMF was instrumental in developing the Special Drawing Rights (SDRs) which were designed to supplement, and perhaps in time to supplant, the other components of international reserves, namely gold and US dollar liabilities. SDRs are created by a deliberate process which takes into account the liquidity needs of the entire international monetary system. Despite some restrictions on their use, SDRs are more like 'owned reserves' as opposed to 'borrowed reserves' that might be created through swap arrangements or IMF credit. After some deliberation, the initial allocation of SDRs was made in January 1970. The allocation for 1970 totalled $3.4 billion, while for 1971 and 1972 annual allocations of $3 billion were made. The distribution of these reserves is based on IMF quotas. Of the total for 1970, $867 million, the largest share, went to the United States while the United Kingdom received the next largest share, $410 million. Canada received $124 million, an amount equal to approximately 4 per cent of its reserves at the end of 1969.

A problem with the SDR scheme is the prospect of conflict over the amount of SDRs to be created. The IMF will continue to play an important role in resolving this conflict through initiating the creation of further allotments. The managing director of the Fund, after consultation with member countries, recommends the amount to be created. An 85 per cent affirmative vote by the Board of Governors of the IMF is required to ratify the managing director's recommendation. As a result, both the United States and the bloc of Common Market countries have effective veto power. Despite some unresolved difficulties concerning the operation of SDRs, the plan is regarded by many as establishing a way of allowing the present international monetary system to continue operating and, perhaps more importantly, to give the IMF a more influential role in the decision-making framework of the system.

Although the IMF did not play a leading role in the establishment of the two-tier gold system, it gave its whole-hearted approval. In the last quarter of 1967 and the first quarter of 1968, speculators purchased about $3 billion of gold on the London gold market as confidence in the pound sterling and the US dollar waned to a new low. At that time and since 1961, the central banks of the gold pool (United States, United Kingdom, Belgium, Germany, Italy, the Netherlands, and Switzerland)[2] had been supporting the private gold market in London in an attempt to maintain the price of gold at $35 an ounce, the official parity of gold to the US dollar. Since speculators periodically expected a devaluation of one of the key currencies, the gold price in London was bid up and the efforts to hold the line forced the central banks of the gold pool to intervene with massive amounts of gold. This reduction in official stocks of gold reinforced the anticipation of the speculators. As a result, hoping to eliminate the chaos thus created, the gold-pool countries disassociated themselves from the London gold market. While the price of $35 an ounce was to be maintained for transactions between the official institutions in settlement of balance-of-payments deficits and surpluses, the price on private gold transactions will be allowed to vary according to market forces. If central banks can be persuaded not to take advantage of profitable arbitrage operations, the destabilizing influence of gold speculation will be removed.

The appropriateness of the International Monetary Fund in meeting the problems of the international financial system as they actually emerged is discussed by Dr Edward Bernstein, formerly director of research of the International Monetary Fund and a member of the American delegation at Bretton Woods. In judging the past accomplishments of the IMF, Bernstein emphasizes the quality of the Fund's thought on problems and policies and its leadership in international monetary co-operation. He argues that the presence of the Fund has enabled the international monetary system to evolve in a number of different ways, including the deliberate creation of reserve assets through SDRs and the promotion of increased co-operation among central banks through swap arrangements and the two-price gold system. However, he finds the evolution less complete with respect to exchange rate policies, techniques of adjustment, and co-ordination of national policies. He is especially worried by the IMF's lack of initiative in 1958 to promote the orderly growth of reserves.

The question remains, however, whether the system even with the introduction of SDRs and the two-price gold system can withstand another buffeting such as it received in 1967 during the pound sterling crisis, in 1969 prior

---

2   France was one of the original members of the gold pool but withdrew in 1967.

to the revaluation of the German mark, and again in 1971 before the realignment of the major currencies. The critics of the present arrangements feel that these reforms only patch up the most obvious faults of the system without getting at the roots of the problem. While some who attended the conference, and many more in the economics community at large, are frustrated by the lack of progress in recognizing the fundamental instability of the Bretton Woods system, Bernstein seems to be convinced that the evolutionary process has been adequate for our needs in the past and will continue to be so in the future.

To many it is a surprise that the World Bank had its origins at Bretton Woods. The Bank is principally linked with the problem of development in the public's mind and it is difficult to imagine that the major countries would have planned for development assistance while they were active in fighting a world war. However, as its formal name implies, the World Bank was originally conceived of as a means of easing the reconstruction problems that would arise when the war was over. Although the formal name also includes the word 'development,' the delegates believed that it would be a long time before the Bank would be able to switch its attention to helping the chronically poor countries.

As events unfolded, the World Bank played only a marginal role in the reconstruction programme. The main instrument of reconstruction was bilateral American aid. Since reconstruction was realized more quickly than was anticipated, the World Bank was free to confront the challenge of aiding development in the less-developed countries. Professor Raymond Mikesell, one of the leading experts on problems of foreign aid and international lending and also a member of the American delegation at Bretton Woods, discusses the suitability of the International Bank for Reconstruction and Development for meeting the problems of financing development. While the IBRD was designed to supplement private capital flows by financing specific projects, the developing countries needed overall development assistance directed to all aspects of social and economic progress. In his paper Mikesell documents the changing emphasis of the Bank from a lending institution to a more comprehensive development agency closer to the needs of the developing countries. The World Bank has brought forth two offspring: the International Development Agency (IDA) and the International Finance Corporation (IFC). Both institutions perform a more specialized role than the World Bank. The IDA, formed in 1960, was designed to provide soft loans to the very poorest of the less-developed countries. In order to reduce the strains of repayment on these countries, the loans are provided on a fifty-year basis with a ten-year grace period and only a three-quarter of 1 per cent service charge per annum. However, the funds of the IDA are small and do not cover the needs of the underdeveloped countries for soft loans. The IFC, in contrast, was established in 1960 in order to provide venture capital to the private sector of the economy of less-developed countries. It either makes loans or buys shares on a minority basis during the early period of the enterprise, hoping to sell its investments to local private interests in an attempt to turn the limited funds over as quickly as possible.

Still further evolution is needed. With the numerous multinational and national foreign assistance agencies, closer co-ordination of programmes is required in the individual recipient countries. The effectiveness of the World Bank's leadership in development assistance depends crucially on its ability to achieve this role as co-ordinator for the individual developing countries. Still, Mikesell's emphasis on the evolution of the World Bank should not be allowed to obscure the primacy of the shortage of aid resources among the problems of development. As the World Bank itself has indicated, between 1965 and 1970 the developing countries could have productively used another $3-4 billion annually beyond what they were receiving in 1965.

Of all the perspectives from which Bretton Woods was viewed, the future posed the greatest potential difficulties for the participants. Clearly, any prediction of the future necessarily involves a firm understanding of the lessons of the past. In many respects the international monetary system has evolved in ways unforeseen by the architects of Bretton Woods. They considered the gains from international trade integration to be far greater than those from international financial integration. They made it acceptable, therefore, to impose controls on capital flows in situations where interference with merchandise flows was not condoned. But the two are not unconnected. The increase in international trade has created a demand for an international means of payment and store of value, a demand which has been largely met by the American dollar. An extensive international credit system, focused on the dollar but involving the financial institutions of many other countries, has evolved, reinforcing, as well as responding to, the emergence of the dollar as the vehicle currency of the world. Capital controls have hindered but not stopped the powerful forces operating to make the dollar dominant. Nevertheless, objections on political grounds have been made by some countries to the extension of American power and influence accompanying the development of the Euro-dollar market and the key-currency status of the dollar.

In a paper with a broad historical scope, Professor Mundell, well known for his imaginative analysis of the international financial system, develops the consequences of the *de facto* evolution of the dollar standard. In his opinion, despite the development of SDRs, the dollar will reveal itself as the most attractive asset for central bankers to hold.

Under any international system there will be a set of adjustment mechanisms that will be allowed to operate. If there is a choice of permitted responses to a problem, the optimal amount of liquidity for that system is the level which induces policy makers to choose the 'best' option. Conceptually there are two problems: deciding the range of choice to be permitted and providing an environment that results in the 'best' option in that range being chosen. Would-be reformers of the system concentrate on both these areas. A number of economists advocate increased flexibility in exchange rates. These proposals vary from wider bands to complete flexibility with a ban on official intervention. Mundell, in his paper, argues that such reforms would not be productive because the increased flow in information and the greater understanding of the consequences of a change in the exchange rate mean the general public will be less willing to accept any reduction in its standard of living through devaluation.

Mundell forsees a system of fixed exchange rates between the developed countries with the American dollar providing both public and private international liquidity. The United States would have an asymmetrical role in the system. Other countries would inflate or deflate to bring their balance of payments into line; the United States would anchor the system by focusing its attention on achieving reasonable price stability. Since the United States would have a responsibility to the world as well as to its own citizens in achieving its objectives, Mundell suggests that the control of American monetary policy would become international.

Several of the points made by Mundell will undoubtedly provoke controversy among economists. Some will disagree with Mundell's interpretation of recent events as indicating a movement closer to a dollar standard. Instead they will interpret the market-determined price of the German mark in 1969 and 1971 and of the Canadian dollar since 1970 as signs of movement toward a system of international monetary arrangements antithetical to both the Bretton Woods agreements and also Mundell's dollar standard. Others will dispute Mundell's denial of the existence of the conditions needed for successful operation of flexible exchange rates. The Canadian experience of 1970 to the present could be cited to illustrate that an orderly movement of the exchange rate is possible. Still, it could be questioned whether the movements of the Canadian dollar have been achieved without official intervention and whether the experience of one relatively small country can be projected to a world of flexible exchange rates. Finally, many economists and, more significantly, many politicians may refuse to accept the surrender of sovereignty implied by Mundell's proposal.

To complement Mundell's paper, Dr Raul Prebisch, formerly secretary-general of the United Nations Conference on Trade and Development and one of the foremost exponents of the cause of the less-developed countries, discusses the ability of the International Monetary Fund and the International Bank for Reconstruction and Development to evolve more effective means of transferring resources to developing countries in the future. Taking up a theme developed by Sir Roy Harrod, he makes a plea for Special Drawing Rights to be used to finance the development requirements of the less-developed countries. The connection between the two issues - aid to economically deprived countries and the creation of an international fiat money - is essentially one of expediency. Those who advocate a distribution of SDRs favouring the less-developed countries feel that every opportunity to increase the transfer of resources to the poor should be exploited. Others argue that such an effort will endanger the acceptability of international money, and that without the successful establishment of SDRs national aid program-mes will be further reduced because of balance-of-payments problems in the donor countries. Those opposed to the linking of the two issues are not necessarily 'anti-development' but believe that both objectives will benefit if they are treated as separate problems.

All perspectives - past, present, and future - on the International Monetary Fund are combined in the address, 'A Report on the Fund,' given by P.P. Schweitzer, managing director of the Fund. After describing the origins of the Fund, Schweitzer assesses the development of the international monetary arrangements under the Fund. He notes a reluctance by countries to change their exchange rates despite provisions for alterations in par values in the Fund charter, and suggests 'there might be advantages in members proposing changes in parities whenever there was substantial evidence of fundamental disequilibrium and without necessarily waiting until such evidence was overwhelming.' In addition, he regrets the gap between understanding and practice in the process of adjustment, in part the result of the political problem of reducing real income in some sectors of the economy. Concluding on an optimistic note, Mr Schweitzer stresses that the con-

tinuation of the constructive spirit of 1944, together with increased understanding of the international financial system, holds the promise of evolutionary change capable of meeting future problems.

On 15 August 1971 the announcement by President Nixon of the temporary suspension of the convertibility of the dollar plunged the international
financial system into its gravest crisis since Bretton Woods. In response to
this measure, coupled with a 10 per cent surcharge on imports, most major
trading countries let their currencies float against the dollar, beginning a
major realignment of par values. Under the aegis of the Group of Ten, a number of meetings of finance ministers and central bank governors were held in
an attempt to resolve the crisis. The United States persisted in refusing to
remove the surcharge except in response to a revaluation of other currencies,
most notably the yen, and certain concessions toward trade liberalism by
members of the European Economic Community. Other countries, especially France, were unwilling to co-operate in any realignment of currencies
without a commitment from the United States to a formal devaluation of
the dollar with respect to gold.

By the beginning of December, after five months and several meetings of
the Group of Ten and other bodies, little progress appeared to have been
made toward any mutually acceptable settlement. Finally, in mid December
following the Nixon-Pompidou summit talks, the Group of Ten reached a
settlement, the so-called Smithsonian Agreement, by which the United
States undertook to devalue the dollar by 7.9 per cent against gold and also
to remove the 10 per cent surcharge. In return, the other countries agreed to
a realignment of other major currencies, with a revaluation against gold of
the Japanese yen by 7.7 per cent and the German mark by 4.6 per cent. The
gold value of the French franc and the British pound remained unchanged.
Of the major currencies, only the Canadian dollar continued to float.

Many of the themes running through the volume emerged as critical issues
in this unsettled phase in the development of the international financial
system. First, the crisis showed up the weakness of the present system of
appointing IMF directors from the middle ranks of the civil service, a practice
criticized by a number of authors in this volume. This weakness was, at least
in part, responsible for the initiative in recent negotiations passing from the
IMF to the Group of Ten, a council of finance ministers and central bank
governors. Second, the initiative toward greater flexibility in exchange rates
taken by P.P. Schweitzer in his paper was reflected in the decision to increase
the range of fluctuation for any currency from 2 per cent to a wider band of

4½ per cent. By far the major question raised by the recent crisis was the future of the dollar in the international financial system. Mundell in his paper, it will be recalled, declared the world had moved to a *de facto* dollar standard. Arguments like Mundell's certainly must have bolstered the Nixon administration's resolve to avoid devaluation of the dollar with respect to gold. As it turned out, such a devaluation has now appeared to be possible without any great trauma. On the other hand, Mundell's interpretation gains support by the lack of any apparent movement toward replacing the dollar as either the currency of intervention or as the major vehicle currency for foreign trade and finance. It should also be noted that the combination of trade and financial matters among the issues at stake has served to underline the criticism by some participants of the artificial separation of trade and finance that has characterized policy since Bretton Woods.

What then is the verdict on the Bretton Woods arrangements after a quarter century? Certainly both institutions have had important successes in adapting to their changed environment. The IBRD has been able to transform itself from a project lending agency to an overall development institution. Similarly, the IMF has taken a major step toward meeting world liquidity needs through implementing the SDR scheme. Ironically, an assessment after a quarter of a century finds both the IBRD and IMF at critical points in their development. With the continuing importance of bilateral aid, the IBRD may find its most important role as co-ordinator of diverse programmes of development assistance. Similarly, with the international monetary system at the crossroads between the dollar standard and increased exchange rate flexibility, the future position of the IMF in the system hinges on its ability to provide leadership. Perhaps a final judgment can never be made of these institutions whose milieu is capable of such sudden and dramatic change.

A.L.K. Acheson
J.F. Chant
M.F.J. Prachowny

BRETTON WOODS REVISITED

PART 1 MEMORIES AND HISTORIES

Sir Roy Harrod

PROBLEMS PERCEIVED IN THE INTERNATIONAL FINANCIAL SYSTEM

I have little doubt that the birth of the two great institutions at Bretton Woods will be recorded in history as a notable landmark in human affairs. The progress towards more orderly international relations on a world scale, and towards having institutions particularly adapted to maintaining such relations, will surely proceed, whatever setbacks we may still have to face on the forward journey. At some future time historians will look back to the state of affairs when the world was divided into a number of independent sovereign states as a curious episode. I hasten to add that I do not believe that mankind will move towards having a world sovereign state that in the least resembles the national sovereign states of today. The national sovereign states have taken many different forms, and within a not very long period we have also had the city states and the feudal system which had quite different characteristics. At present we happen to think in terms of a democratically elected legislature, an executive, and a judiciary. I do not believe that this will ever be duplicated on a world scale. It must be remembered that man is flexible and malleable in his ideas, and that these can be adapted to various kinds of social relations and institutions. What the nature of those will be we have not at present the remotest idea. If we did have, we might adopt them right away! Man is inventive; but his powers of invention take time to evolve.

If this outline of a wider context is correct, that makes the International Monetary Fund and the International Bank for Reconstruction and Development all the more interesting. They are structurally different from the traditional organizations of national states and may give us some inkling as to what the world-wide international institutions that are destined to bring human affairs into better order will be like. The Bretton Woods Conference will be a great landmark, because it set up two international institutions that have been in effective operation for a quarter of a century and are surely destined to have a very long life indeed. There have been and are, of course, other international organizations, such as the League of Nations before even World War II. But it would be difficult to find other organizations as well constructed to fulfil their various functions as are the IMF and the IBRD.

In what follows I do not propose to confine myself to wide generalities, but rather I shall deal, to the best of my ability, with a number of particular matters. That being so, I feel that it is appropriate to mention very briefly my credentials for doing so, since not all that I say will necessarily be agreed to by everyone.

I may mention, first, that in the dozen years before Bretton Woods I was observing the international economic scene from the standpoint of someone who had already published work on such matters. This may seem rather a feeble claim, but, alas, the number who can make it is dwindling. Secondly, I had much discussion and correspondence with J.M. Keynes over a three-year period concerning his drafts on various subjects which the British eventually put forward in memoranda to the Americans and Canadians in the years prior to Bretton Woods. I was subject to the Official Secrets Act at that time, so Keynes was able to talk quite freely to me on points of detail. Thirdly, I attended many interdepartmental meetings in the British government to determine what the British attitude should be on a number of points and to hammer out various schemes. I suppose that my status at these meetings should be called that of an 'observer.' I represented the private Statistical Branch of the Prime Minister. It was my duty to inform him of what was proceeding in rough outline, and to draw his attention if anything seemed to me to be going amiss.

I was not present at Bretton Woods, nor at any international meetings on the subject, but I visited the United States on two occasions during the war on entirely different business. My position enabled me to discuss international postwar reconstruction 'off the cuff' with a number of American officials.

Thinking at this time was very much influenced by the world slump of 1929-33, from which many economies had not fully recovered at the outbreak of the war in 1939. This was the most severe slump in recorded history. It is a fact worth stressing that thirty-five years later we are still unable to pinpoint its causes — a failure that must give economists and economic historians a sense of modesty. They have multiplied enormously throughout the world in the intervening period and include many persons of great ability. Their tools of research, such as econometric techniques, aided, if necessary, by the computer, have been much improved. Yet despite this, they are unable to answer this very vital question – why did the world slump occur?

In the early phases of the slump, some economists attributed the troubles to the dislocations in the foreign exchanges due to Germany having to make postwar reparations payments. In retrospect the quantities involved do not seem to have been great enough, and the chain of causation is not clear. Somewhat later the view became prevalent that the cause of the trouble was the Wall Street crash of 1929. It is not certain that this was the principal cause, and even if we judged that it was, this merely pushes the problem one stage further back – what caused the supernormal boom in Wall Street and in other forms of speculation, in real estate, for example, in 1929? In relation to 'boom and bust' it is to be noted that, apart from finance, the United States economy had not shown many signs of what we now call 'over-heating' in the years prior to the crash. Commodity prices were not rising, and unemployment was reported to be considerable. The Federal Reserve System had begun to have some success in ironing out the business cycle.

Furthermore, there were symptoms of a tendency to recession outside the US prior to the crash. Thus it is possible that the fundamental cause lay outside the US, or that it was due to some lack of balance in the world as a whole including the US. The uncertainty about the true causes has to be borne in mind in considering later views about needful recipes. Thinking prior to Bretton Woods was influenced by the desire that the world should not be plunged again into heavy unemployment after World War II was over.

Study of the World Economic Conference of 1933 in London is relevant to the pre-Bretton Woods discussions. In consequence of difficulties caused by the slump many countries had by then adopted stringent measures of protection by way of tariffs, import quotas, and exchange controls. The prevailing thought at the London Conference was that the prime cure for the troubles should be a concerted effort by the nations to get rid of the obstacles to trade. Keynes (who was not a member of the conference) took a different view. Shortly before the conference he contributed articles to *The Times* and the *New Statesman and Nation*; these were collected into a booklet entitled *The Means to Prosperity*. He took the line that the restrictions on trade had been the consequence and not the cause of the troubles:

For the Conference to occupy itself with pious resolutions concerning the abatement of tariffs, quotas and exchange restrictions would be a waste of time. Insofar as these things are not the expression of deliberate national or imperial policies they have been adopted reluctantly as a means of self-protection and are symptoms, not causes, of the tension on the foreign exchanges. It is dear to the heart of Conferences to pass pious resolutions deploring symptoms while leaving the disease untouched.

What did Keynes think the disease was? He believed, of course, that, on a world scale, there was insufficient investment to match the propensity to save and that the remedy was a concerted effort to get more investment going in all countries. It was essential that investments, to the extent that they were undertaken by the public authorities, should, like private investment, be financed by *loans*, and not by taxation. He was not much in favour of international loans — those representing the World Bank must forgive me — since he always saw danger in the build-up of international indebtedness. He did, however, in the end put his authority and his power of persuasion behind the IBRD. He wanted the various countries to start their development schemes and stressed the importance of the 'multiplier effect' of these on the general level of demand and consumption.

But how about the balance-of-payments problems of the various countries during the recovery process? For this he recommended the setting up of an international authority for the issue of gold notes, of which the face value would be expressed in terms of the gold content of the dollar. He suggested that these notes should be issued up to a maximum of $5000 million. It is interesting to note the size of this figure. In ratio to the trade of today a comparable figure would be something more than $35,000 million. (Those concerned with the SDR proposal might take note of this.) In arriving at this figure of $35,000 million, I have been careful to compare the present day with 1928 and not with 1933, so as to avoid a ratio based on the extremely depressed condition of international trade in the latter year. In relation to SDRs the following quotation is apposite: 'It' [that is, the international money] 'should not be of an eleemosynary character, but should be available not only to the exceptionally needy but to all participating countries in accordance with a general formula. Indeed, there are few, if any, countries left today which are so entirely without anxiety that they would not like some strengthening of their position.'

Gold is somewhat under discussion today, and before leaving Keynes' thought at the time of the World Economic Conference of 1933 it may be interesting to quote his views:

In the first place the additional reserves should be based on gold. For whilst gold is rapidly ceasing to be national money, it is becoming, even more exclusively than before, the international money most gladly held in reserve and used to meet a foreign drain ... There remains one essential condition. The notes would be gold notes, and the participants would agree to accept them as the equivalent of gold. This implies that the national currencies of each participant would stand in some defined relationship to gold. It involves, that is to say, a qualified return to the gold standard. It may seem odd that I, who have lately described gold as a 'barbarous relic,' should be discovered as an advocate of such policy, at a time when the orthodox authorities of this country are laying down conditions for our return to gold which they must know to be impossible of fulfilment. It may be that never having loved gold I am not so subject to disillusion. But, mainly, it is because I believe that gold has received such a gruelling that conditions might now be laid down for its future management which would not have been acceptable otherwise.

He also laid down that 'Each participating country should adopt a *de facto* parity between gold and its national currency, with buying and selling points for gold separated by not more than five per cent.' Finally, I cannot forebear to quote from this booklet a sentence relating to a different subject: 'Nor should it seem strange that taxation may be so high as to defeat its object, and that, given sufficient time to gather the fruits, a reduction of taxation will run a better chance than an increase of balancing the Budget.' It might have been Mr Walter Heller speaking.

There was another person who was not on the same wavelength as the World Economic Conference — President Roosevelt. During the course of the conference he sent over a message that the US was dealing with the problem of the depression in a somewhat different way (including raising the price of gold) and would not be ready to join with others in a free trade move at that time. This message was widely held to have sabotaged the conference.

The American Smoot-Hawley tariff of 1930, the root causes of which, however, had nothing to do with the slump, was not very helpful to the cause of free trade. In due course the American scene changed through the vigorous efforts of Cordell Hull to make mutual agreements for tariff reductions — efforts which had a good measure of success. Hull's influence was very important in the wartime discussions between the US and the UK which led up to Bretton Woods.

In relation to these discussions, three important landmarks should be mentioned in temporal order.

1 Herr Funk had been making propaganda in German-occupied territories with a document called 'The New Order,' which described the brave new world that the Nazis would have to offer when the war was over. Keynes had the idea of writing a counterblast indicating that the British Commonwealth would be able to offer something better. It was not thought wise to publish this, but Keynes brought the draft with him on his first wartime visit to the US in 1941 and showed it to various officials there. The American reaction was that the British should not think of themselves as going it alone when the war was over; the Americans would wish to join in providing the means of establishing a better world economic order. The Americans immediately got busy thinking about this problem.

2 Quite soon after this, there occurred the meeting between Winston Churchill and President Roosevelt which resulted in the issue of the Atlantic Charter.

3 Closely connected with this, but having a somewhat different origin, was the presentation by the Americans to the British of what was known as the 'Consideration.'

Early in 1941 the newly re-elected President Roosevelt devised a scheme for helping the British. It could be operated despite the stern legislation by Congress enacted shortly after Britain ceased making payments on its World War I debt to the US against giving credits to belligerents. (War debt was another phenomenon connected with the world slump.) The President had the idea of lending or leasing to Britain objects that might be useful to the war effort. 'When one's neighbour's house is on fire one lends him a hose-pipe.' No dollar sign was to be put on the objects thus lent, in order to avoid undesirable pressures and dislocations in the foreign exchanges when the war should be over. But the question was soon raised – would it make sense for Britain to return the physical objects, such as aircraft of design by then probably obsolete, or tobacco? Thoughts arising out of the foregoing problems, namely Anglo-American co-operation to produce a better world than Herr Funk was likely to be able to manage, and thoughts resulting from the solemn declaration of the Atlantic Charter suggested a somewhat different procedure. Why should not the British, in 'consideration' for the aircraft and tobacco which were currently being, or were about to be, provided to them, repay, not in kind, but by co-operating with the Americans on certain lines of policy favoured by them. The main point in the first draft of the 'Consideration' shown to the British was the elimination of 'discrimination' in foreign commercial policy. Cordell Hull had especially in mind British 'imperial preference,' a particular bugbear of his. In consequence of British representations to the Americans that this would not be a 'winner' in Britain, the Americans very much broadened the basis of the proposed Consideration as follows:

In the final determination of the benefits to be provided to the United States of America by the Government of the United Kingdom in return for Lend-Lease aid, the terms and conditions thereof shall be such as not to burden commerce between the two countries, but to promote mutually advantageous economic relations between them and the betterment of world-wide economic relations. To that end, they shall include provision for agreed action by the United States of America and the United Kingdom, open to participation by all other countries of like mind, directed to the expansion, by appropriate international and domestic measures of production, employment, and the exchange and consumption of goods, which are the material foundations of the liberty and welfare of all peoples; to the elimination of all forms of discriminatory treatment in international commerce, and to the reduction of tariffs and other trade barriers; and, in general, to the attainment of all the economic objectives set forth in the Atlantic Charter.

Thus discrimination still figured, but in a comparatively minor way. What the subsequent interpretation of it was to be in relation to imperial preference was settled by a direct interchange between Winston Churchill and President Roosevelt.

Both the British and Americans got to work on how to effect a better world order. On the American side, the thinking of Cordell Hull continued to be important. One of his aides was Leo Pasvolsky, and he in turn was in close liaison with a member of the British Embassy in Washington, Redvers Opie, who kept the British well informed about what dire things might happen if they did not align their thinking to that of Cordell Hull. But there was also other thinking on the American side. Mention must be made of Harry White and his able lieutenant Eddy Bernstein. Mr White was busy at an early stage devising drafts for international institutions on the lines that eventuated in the IMF and the IBRD. In the course of his proceedings there was a certain interchange of functions between the two institutions.

British thinking was very much influenced by Keynes. His ideas remained similar to those he had propounded in *Means to Prosperity*. He thought in terms of an international authority to issue gold notes and of the adoption by various countries of domestic policies to ensure full employment – in contrast with the dismal prewar record. Already in 1941 he had made a number of drafts of what was eventually to be published under the title of a Clearing Union. At first the majority view in the UK was that Britain should be very cautious about committing itself to dismantling its protective devices, as obviously it would have heavy balance-of-payments difficulties when the war was over. The British could argue that other European countries, which one would wish to bring in as co-operators in the scheme for a better world would also have similar problems at such a time; it was a British duty to think of them, as they were currently represented only by expatriate governments, if at all. It can probably be said that in 1941 the majority of British politicians and top civil servants would have taken the line that Britain should find diplomatic means for not committing themselves to the doctrines of the Consideration. Hubert Henderson, who still had more influence at that time in the British Treasury than Keynes, was violently opposed to Britain's acceptance. Keynes, even while composing his drafts of the Clearing Union, was still in doubt. An official visit by Alvin Hansen helped matters along. He proposed the establishment of an international economic board to advise collaborating governments on internal policies to promote full employment, economic stability, and world trade; an international resources survey; and an international development corporation. All this was very much in line with the *Means to Prosperity* and it even impressed Hubert Henderson who, although against free trade, favoured such stimulants as public works.

Keynes had to convince first himself and then ultimately others that the British should agree to go along with America on commercial policy on condition that the Americans on their side would agree to a scheme for the establishment of an international institution to issue gold notes, which he at first called Grammor and later Bancor, on a generous scale. Thus there was to be a trade-off between the British adopting Cordell Hull's ideas and the Americans agreeing to something like the International Monetary Fund. Meanwhile, unbeknown to the British, Harry White and his associates were already working on similar schemes for increasing international liquidity. Mr White had submitted successive drafts to those concerned in the US.

In consequence of the persuasive power of Keynes and the power position of the US, although this was temporarily reduced by Pearl Harbour, Britain did come round to the idea of this trade-off; and the Mutual Aid Agreement, which was the liberalized version of the Consideration, was signed in February 1942. Oddly enough, when Churchill visited the US after Pearl Habour he was unable to get Roosevelt to discuss the subject; the matter had to be settled between them by subsequent communications. I may be permitted to add that his Statistical Branch was briefing Churchill in the right way.

The British organized a meeting of the dominions in the later part of 1942 at which only Canada played an active role. Mr Rasminsky is especially remembered in this connection. The Canadians were also present at the all-important meeting in Washington in September 1943, where the main lines of the proposals to be put forward at Bretton Woods were agreed to. There was a further interchange of correspondence and discussion between relevant people during the winter of 1943-4.

Britain formulated an agenda for postwar reconstruction under four heads: international monetary arrangements, international investment, buffer stocks in primary commodities, and commercial policy. It was the British view that the Americans should play the main part in devising what we now know as the World Bank, since it was they alone who would be able to afford to give it generous financial support after the war. Keynes himself was, as I have already stated, not very keen on international investment, holding that the indebtedness thereby created was dangerous in relation to the balance of payments of the recipient countries. (We may think of India at the present day.) He would doubtless have favoured IDA strongly, as compared with the more orthodox operations of the IBRD. At the eleventh hour, however, in the final journey across the Atlantic Ocean before Bretton Woods, he became quite an enthusiast for a world bank and made a notable speech at the prior meeting in Atlantic City.

He attached particular importance to the buffer stock scheme; but this was not established at the Washington meeting (1943) as part of the agenda for Bretton Woods; it was ground down between the upper and lower millstones of two conflicting American views. One was that of Henry Wallace and his coadjutors who thought that it would interfere too much with American domestic agricultural policy as needed to sustain American farming. The other was the more orthodox one, represented by persons like Will Clayton, who thought that world commodity prices should be established by world market forces. For one who remembers vividly how enthusiastic was Keynes on the buffer stock scheme, it is good news that the IMF and the IBRD are both, a quarter of a century later, thinking purposefully about buffer stock plans.

Despite initial doubts, the British had, now that it seemed probable that something like the International Monetary Fund would be accepted, become more friendly to American ideas about commercial policy. This was partly due to the notable groundwork done by Professor James Meade. The plans for this went elsewhere and are now to a limited extent enshrined in the GATT. In this paper we are concerned only with the first two items on the British agenda.

I should summarize the ways in which thinking about postwar problems actuated the Bretton Woods plans. The main objective was to prevent a relapse into a world-wide slump. The recipe most strongly recommended by one school of thought was to prevent nations reverting to cut-throat protectionism. This was accepted, with limitations, and ultimately became part of the GATT and, in the field of monetary restriction, is reflected in the Articles of Agreement of the IMF. The other school laid greater stress on the need for concerted development plans. The IBRD looks after part of this programme, but another essential part is managed by the IMF, *both* in respect of providing more liquidity to tide nations over developmental periods causing a balance-of-payments problem, *and* to enable nations which have become victims of demand, or cost-push, inflation to overcome their difficulties by the use of the 'adjustable peg' without having to impose domestic restraints throttling growth and causing unemployment as was required by the unreformed gold standard.

A few words might be said about how this has worked out. I propose to do this in relation to (I) theory and (II) practical devices.

I

In my citations from Keynes's *Means to Prosperity* I did not reveal that one of his prime objectives was to get a rise of prices from the woefully unprofitable level to which they had fallen in 1933. In 1944 it was thought that they would again collapse when the war was over. It could be argued that we now live in quite a different world, in which one of the greatest evils is persistent price inflation and there is not much serious unemployment.

The Keynes doctrines are logically symmetrical. Thus, in this very different world we are said to be 'all good Keynesians' if we adopt damping measures to prevent excess demand, over-full employment, and price inflation. I do not believe that, if Keynes were alive, he would have interpreted the matter in this way at all. I feel sure that he would have revised his views on this topic, as he was continually doing during his lifetime; but always with unchanged basic ideas. His mind was very flexible and able to learn from experience. In the *Economic Consequences of the Peace* (1919) he lambasted inflation, quite correctly at the time, and 'quoted' Lenin — there is current controversy as to whether this is a correct 'quotation' — as being reported to have said that the surest way of destroying capitalism was to have inflation. Within a couple of years he was saying that deflation was probably a greater evil than inflation.

I will now set out three propositions. They are probably incorrect as universals, but true in certain circumstances, and probably in many countries in present circumstances. They contradict the 'conventional wisdom' taught in most universities. But pure economic theory has nothing against them.

1 Raising taxes, whether direct or indirect, is inflationary, because its effect in causing price quotations, based on cost, to be raised is stronger than the downward affect, if any, that reducing aggregate demand has on prices.

2 High interest rates are inflationary, because their entry into costs has more effect on prices than has their effect in reducing aggregate demand.

3 Damping demand itself, except in cases where at existing prices it is running in excess of the supply potential of the economy (as, for example, it is obviously not doing in the UK at present), is price-inflationary, except, perhaps, in a very short period, because it raises unit costs of production.

I repeat that there is nothing in pure economic theory that would invalidate these three propositions. Their validity in relation to economics at a given period and in given countries can be verified, or falsified, only by econometric study and field work. I will concede that reduction of aggregate demand is normally price-deflationary, but often, again, only in the short period, in the case of commodities marketed in conditions of perfect competition. But these have come to play a much smaller part in the flow of goods and services in advanced countries. It may be that the too ready acceptance of propositions of contrary sense to those that I have just recited is a hangover from an earlier period when conditions were different.

I turn to another aspect — the less-developed countries. The sixties were supposed ironically to be the 'developing decade' designed to stimulate help for them. In fact this decade has been sadly laggard in this respect. To what extent is this due to important buyers of their products, like the UK, having damped their economies in order to check their own price inflations and improve their balances of payments? Incidentally, this policy has been a signal failure in the UK in respect of both those objectives. It is a matter for investigation how far stronger growth in some industrial countries would have helped the less developed countries in recent years.

Whether more expansionist policies in some industrial countries would have helped much or little, it is not likely that they would have fully solved the problems of the poorer countries. Accordingly, other methods should be sought within the framework, not of the actual institutions as they are now working, but within the framework of the ideologies of their founders. Those founders did not conceive their work as providing the final answer for all time, but only as a beginning.

There is much to be said for the plan devised by Max Stamp, by which the original issue of gold notes each year would be channelled through the IBRD to finance developments in the less-developed countries without their incurring any repayment obligations. Those countries would use the 'notes' provided to them in order to purchase capital goods from the industrial countries, and the notes would thus pass into general circulation, supplementing international liquidity. It might be difficult to draw a line between the less-developed countries and the rest. To remove an eleemosynary stigma and reduce the matter to a general formula, one might make the amount of issue to each country per caput inversely proportional to its gross national product per caput. This would make it equivalent to a negative income tax such as now being discussed on a domestic basis in some countries.

Then there are the buffer stock plans. Devised in the first instance to iron out price oscillations, they should, it has been suggested, be used to sustain prices at a remunerative level for a given quantum of production, presumably with the quantum rising year by year in accordance with requirements. The price as thus sustained might be above the economic price, and this feature should in that case be regarded as a bridging measure only, pending the time when the countries relying mainly on the export of primary products had a more diversified bill of fare to offer in world markets.

And how might that come about? Here we might have to go over to the GATT rules, with the IMF, however, watching on the touchline. One might think of the industrial countries giving strong tariff preferences to the imports of manufactures from the less-developed countries. Even these might not avail, owing to the narrow domestic markets of those countries which prevent their having sufficient economies of scale, and to their lack of know-how in selling around the world. To remedy this, one might think of long-term bulk purchase agreements between the industrial and the less-developed countries, whether on a bilateral or multilateral basis, whereby the latter might be put on their feet as exporters of manufactures on a substantial scale and, in due course, at economic prices. These proposals do not conform precisely to the existing principles and rules of the international agencies. But I submit that they conform to the ideology of at least some of those who were responsible for establishing them.

II

The British plan for a trade-off between more liberal commercial policies and American agreement to a scheme for supplementing the amount of international liquidity has not worked out. The British did in due course go forward, too boldly and quickly in my opinion, with the policy of dismantling import controls. But the quantity of world reserves in ratio to international dealings has not in fact risen but has shrunk grievously, whether we compare with 1937-8 or 1928. This is entirely contrary to what was intended at the time of Bretton Woods.

The main reason for this perverse outcome has been the failure to raise the price of gold in terms of all currencies in line with the universal rise in the currency prices of other goods. Whether such a rise in the price of gold at the appropriate time alone would have sufficed, taken in conjunction with the increased use of reserve currencies and with facilities at the IMF to fulfil its founders' intention that total world reserves should be supplemented, is not possible to say. The reason is that one cannot assess the effect of such a rise in the price of gold on its production, on its use as a medium of liquid reserve by persons or corporations other than central banks — often referred to, wrongly in my opinion, as 'hoarding' — or on its use for industrial purposes.

My next point concerns the scarce currency clause in the Articles of Agreement of the IMF (Article VII). The clause has not been used, although there have been occasions when its use would have been appropriate, in accordance with the intentions of the founders. Its non-use may have been well advised. The great progress that has been made since 1945 towards larger freedom of multilateral, non-discriminatory trade might have surprised the founders of the IMF. The scarce currency clause in its essence entails discrimination. The need for the clause arose out of the fact that, at one time or another, the sum total of the quotas of members in debit in their external dealings might exceed the sum total of the quotas of the members in credit. Provided that the members in debit were able to satisfy the Fund that they were conducting their affairs in an appropriate manner, they would be entitled to draw. But the Fund would lack the wherewithal to honour this entitlement. It could meet the situation by declaring the currency of one or more creditor countries 'scarce.' If use of the scarce currency clause is ruled out on ideological grounds and no other arrangement is made, the Fund becomes insolvent. It was to meet this situation that Per Jacobsson devised the General Arrangements to Borrow, which have been used. This has put the Group of Ten into a power position vis-à-vis the Fund — which, however harmonious the practical working may be, is in principle open to criticism.

Finally, I will mention Article IV, which gives members the right, subject to the agreement of the Fund, except for a once-only movement of 10 per cent, to alter their exchange rates in the event of a 'fundamental disequilibrium.' This is commonly known as the adjustable peg. The existence of this right has, since the general restoration of the convertibility of currencies, caused corporations from time to time to make very large movements of funds in order to protect their positions in the event of a country choosing to exert the right within the relevant time horizon. Under the gold standard it was considered dishonourable for a country to alter its gold parity; it would be rather like an individual going bankrupt. Article IV has rendered devaluation respectable and therefore not wildly improbable for a respectable country in a balance-of-payments difficulty. Under a system of flexible exchange rates, such as is now being discussed in some quarters, the rate would at any time stand at a level at which there were as many advisers to corporations who thought a given currency likely to move upwards within the relevant time horizon as thought it likely to move down. By contrast, under the adjustable peg system, the expectation in relation to a given currency is that it will be moved downwards or not at all. I need hardly add that the expectation that it may be moved upwards or not all can give rise to an equally large one-way movement of precautionary funds.

These movements of funds on precautionary account, to which the unacademic epithet of 'vast' may appropriately be applied, have been looked after by the co-operation of central banks in providing mutual standby swap credits, progressively increased, or by *ad hoc* credits, to offset them. The sums are much larger than could comfortably be looked after, or are even intended to be looked after, by the IMF, and much larger than the countries affected could look after, given the exiguous present level of world reserves. This system of mutual support has in most cases worked very smoothly and indeed may be esteemed a shining example of the growth of co-operativeness among nations, or, at least, among their central bankers, in recent years. But the system is not what might be called ship-shape.

We have three authorities, independent in theory but only partly so in practice, for making the world monetary system continue to tick over — the IMF, the Group of Ten, and the more informal group of central bankers, who meet, more often than not, at Basel.

Although I have made some critical remarks, and I hope that criticism is more worthy of this great occasion than a flow of anodyne platitudes, I should like to affirm that human welfare in the world would have been substantially less had it not been for the existence of the IMF and the IBRD. These have functioned effectively. The world without them would have been considerably poorer. But on this occasion of a silver jubilee I would suggest that it is proper for the world, taking its cue from Queen's University, to consider the problem of a little restructuring. As regards the IBRD I would think that the main emphasis should be towards making the IDA a major element, in order to avoid the increasing burden of international indebtedness. To such an enlargement of the IDA, countries would have to consent to be heavy contributors. Thus in a sense the IBRD problem is more serious than that of the IMF, which merely needs a re-thinking of principles, leading to a certain restructuring.

Which is more difficult — to raise more money or to re-think principles? To re-think principles is more difficult.

Richard N. Gardner

THE POLITICAL SETTING

'History,' it has been said, 'is lived forward but is written in retrospeçt. We know the end before we know the beginning and we can never wholly recapture what it was to know the beginning only.' It is difficult to reconstruct the intellectual, political, and economic setting of the Bretton Woods Conference a quarter of a century later. But it is useful to try. The effort may help explain the international financial system we have inherited from the past – and it may even tell us something about the steps we can take to improve that system today. According to the old cliché, those who ignore history are condemned to repeat it. I doubt that this is any less true in the field of international monetary policy than in other areas.

Perhaps the first important thing to note at the outset is that the Bretton Woods Conference and the crucial negotiations that preceded it were very much an Anglo-American affair, with Canada playing a useful mediating role. For historical reasons that were unique, these three countries had an unusually large influence in the negotiations. Germany, Italy, and Japan, countries that today hold a large measure of economic power, were then enemy countries and thus not represented at Bretton Woods. France was still under German occupation; its government-in-exile played only a marginal role. The less-developed countries played nothing like the part they play today in international economic conferences. The Soviet Union came only at the last minute and sat on the sidelines.

The United States, of course, was the dominant element. For better or worse only the US had the resources to make these institutions work. Moreover – and people often forget this in recalling the Bretton Woods Conference – the war was still on. The Normandy landings took place only a month before the conference opened. The allies had not yet broken out of the Normandy beachhead; nobody knew when the war would end or how it would be won. There was almost complete dependence on the United States militarily, politically, and economically. No wonder, then, that the US role at Bretton Woods was decisive. It is unlikely that there will ever be another world conference in which American power is so preponderant.

Since the United States' role was so decisive at Bretton Woods, it is worth examining in some detail the political and economic factors that influenced the American delegation. The US negotiators operated with certain basic preconceptions. One was that the mistakes made after the First World War must be avoided. To begin with, this meant that planning for the postwar period should begin early – indeed, it began as early as 1941 and 1942. Secondly, the United States should join a system of world organizations and play a leading part in building a new world order. Unfortunately, thinking about the kind of world in which international organizations would operate tended to be somewhat naive. Cordell Hull, for example, could say at the time of Bretton Woods that once a United Nations was created, 'there will no longer be need for spheres of influence, for alliances, for balance of power, or any other of the special arrangements through which, in the unhappy past, nations strove to safeguard their security or to promote their interests.'[1] Harry White described as follows the assumptions under which he laboured in wartime Washington:

It was expected that the early post-war world would witness a degree of unity and good-will in international political relationships among the victorious allies never before reached in peace time. It was expected that the world would move rapidly ... toward 'One World' ... No influential persons, as far as I can remember, expressed the expectation or the fear that international relations would worsen during these years.

The widely shared assumption, in other words, was that there would be a new political deal – 'one world' – with power somehow exorcised from the system. There was no anticipation of the cold war. Nobody foresaw the need for huge US overseas expenditures for military defence and foreign aid; no one foresaw the magnitude of Britain's overseas spending. The working-papers for the Anglo-American financial negotiations in the fall of 1945 es-

1 References for this quotation and the others that follow may be found in my *Sterling-Dollar Diplomacy* (2nd edition, 1969).

timated British government overseas expenditures after the transitional period at $250 million. (British overseas government expenditures were seven times that by the early 1960s.) The political assumptions behind Bretton Woods were thus very far from the postwar realities.

A related element in US thinking was the preoccupation with economics — with the economic basis of a durable peace. Here again the postwar planners drew lessons from the interwar history. Profoundly influenced by the writings of Keynes and others, they believed the Versailles settlement had collapsed because of its inadequate economic foundation. They were determined not to make that mistake again. This time there would be an adequate economic underpinning for the postwar arrangements.

The emphasis on economics was welcome up to a point; but it tended to be overdone. Leo Pasvolsky, for example, stated that unwillingness to abandon policies of economic warfare would constitute 'the *greatest* danger that will confront us after the war' (emphasis added). Arthur Krock, summarizing the mood in Washington at the time, said 'economic freedom for all is the basic American foreign policy for the prevention of war.' The old cliché, 'if goods can't cross borders, soldiers will,' seemed to underline much of the thinking of the State Department under Cordell Hull. The Secretary of State actually believed that the fundamental causes of the world wars lay in economic discrimination and trade warfare. Some of his aides went so far as to propose a trade agreement with Nazi Germany in 1939 as a means of avoiding the Second World War!

Another element in American thinking was the very great emphasis on the concept of multilateralism or non-discrimination in trade and payments. The US was preoccupied with the imperial preference system. (The US in those days was on an anti-imperialist crusade. It is ironic to note that twenty-five years later the US is the country most on the receiving end of this charge.) Economic spheres of influence were regarded as a threat to peace, and particularly to the American concept of 'one world.' The Ottawa Agreements were also considered very harmful to American trade interests.

There was also a strong American desire to get rid of exchange controls and quotas. Here the US commitment was not to free trade as such, but rather to preserve a role for the price mechanism. Thus, tariffs were permissible, but not direct controls. The concept was practical as well as ideological. The US wanted an environment in which American trade could expand — in which the comparative advantage of the United States in key sectors could make its impact, free from unreasonable burdens and restrictions.

Still another element — one that looks particularly curious in retrospect — was the strong feeling of many of the New Dealers against bankers. Henry Morgenthau proudly declared at Bretton Woods that the Fund and Bank would 'drive the usurious money lenders from the temple of international finance.' (It would be interesting to know what Morgenthau thought in the very final months of his life when the 'usurious money lenders' led by the Federal Reserve Bank of New York mobilized several billion dollars in forty-eight hours to rescue sterling.) The close collaboration between central bankers and governments that has characterized the postwar period was neither foreseen nor even encouraged by the wartime planners. Indeed, at US initiative, the Bretton Woods Conference adopted a resolution asking the Bank for International Settlements to go out of existence.

A particularly important feature of the American setting that needs to be noted was the rivalry between the Treasury and the State Department. Treasury had the upper hand because Morgenthau was a close friend of President Roosevelt. This helps explain why primacy was given to the financial side of postwar planning. (Had Hull been Roosevelt's Dutchess County neighbour instead of Morgenthau, we might have ended up with an ITO and not an IMF!) Another result of the division between State and Treasury was that problems of trade and finance were dealt with in virtually water-tight compartments. These divisions were carried over into our international economic organizations, with results that still afflict us. It is anomalous that if a country is in balance-of-payments difficulty and resorts to trade restrictions — quotas or import surcharges — its problems are discussed in GATT, while if it comes for financial aid or employs exchange controls, its problems are discussed in the IMF. There is no adequate co-ordination or integration of policy between these two institutions. This is traceable right back to the divisions within the US executive branch during World War II.

So far I have concentrated on the executive branch. What about Congress and the public at large? We tend now to forget the lingering isolationist tradition that was still very strong at the time of Bretton Woods. It was a tremendous undertaking to bring the United States into the IMF and Bank. Up to that time the United States had not joined any universal world organization. There was real doubt that the American Congress would approve membership in international financial organizations, or even in the United Nations itself.

There was also a strong *laissez-faire* tradition, which complicated the task of bringing the US into the Fund and Bank. It is extraordinary to re-read some of the things that were said at the time about the White plan and the Keynes plan in the press and in the US financial community. The Guaranty Trust Company, for example, could say that both the Keynes and White plans were 'dangerous' because they would 'enable nations to buy merchandise without being able to pay for it' and would 'substitute fallible human judgment and discretion for the impersonal action of the markets in regulating balances of international payments and foreign exchange rates.' The American Bankers Association declared that 'a system of quotas or shares in a pool which gives debtor countries the impression that they have a right to credits up to some amount is unsound in principle, and raises hopes that cannot be realized.' *The New York Times* thought neither plan was necessary because 'the gold standard was, without any international agreements, the most satisfactory international standard that has ever been devised.'

There was, finally, the pervasive feeling that the United States was the world's perennial surplus country and had to protect itself against too liberal access to international credits. Senator Taft rose on the floor of the Senate to complain that the United States was 'putting ... all the valuable money in the Fund' and that US participation would mean 'pouring money down a rat hole.' The US negotiators did not hold these extreme views, but they had to take account of them. Moreover, even they may have been victims of an 'arrogance of power' when it came to economics; they hardly imagined that the US might some day need international assistance in dealing with its own payments problems.

Let us look now at the other side of the Atlantic – at the political and economic setting in Britain. Several factors were working on behalf of cooperation with the US in a postwar financial arrangement. The most obvious was the complete British dependence on the United States. This was not a negotiation between equals or between two fully independent countries. The United States was giving $30 billion of lend-lease aid to Britain; there was no equivalent British leverage on the United States. In the last analysis the British had to accept what the Americans wanted. But there were also reasons based on Britain's own perceived self-interest for working with the US for the kind of economic system envisaged at Bretton Woods. British opinion was strongly committed to the concept of world organization in the economic as well as in the political field. The liberal economic tradition still had a good deal of vitality. Academics in government like James Meade and Lionel Robbins, civil servants like Richard Hopkins, ministers like Richard Law, were committed to liberal economic principles. Keynes, as Sir Roy Harrod has brought out so brilliantly in his biography, was doubtful at first, but came around to a liberal approach on the assurance of a generous liquidity package and an American commitment to help in British reconstruction.

Yet throughout the negotiations there were three important British reservations. The first was a concern — one might almost say a fixation — with full employment. The trauma of the 1930s had a profound effect on British thinking: freedom to maintain full employment at home had to be safeguarded in any postwar financial plan. No one today would quarrel with that as an objective, but re-reading British comments of a generation ago one is struck by the extent to which this one theme was exalted over all others. Herbert Morrison could say, for example, that 'one of the biggest contributions' Britain could make to world trade after the war would be to 'have a *shortage* of labour' (emphasis added). The British government could argue in international meetings that full employment was 'the main condition for the maintenance of satisfactory levels of living.' Very little, if anything, was said about employment being *productive* as well as *full* — and even less was said about how the necessary productivity could be achieved. Keynes sometimes talked as if exchange rate changes by themselves could provide a satisfactory method of adjustment. He told the House of Commons that under the Bretton Woods agreement the external value of sterling could be altered 'to conform to whatever *de facto* internal value results from domestic policies which themselves shall be immune from criticism.' Not only during the wartime period but for years thereafter, the focus of political discussion in Britain was on the responsibilities which the United States would have to undertake to restore equilibrium to Britain's balance of payments. It would have been better for all concerned if equal efforts had been given to educating the British people on British responsibilities for restoring equilibrium. (The failure to do this has proved costly. Keynes would have thought it incredible if someone had told him the hard facts of the 1960s — that the United Kingdom would run huge balance-of-payments deficits when the United States was also running huge balance-of-payments deficits. The British leaders simply assumed that if the United States ran deficits, Britain would run surpluses, and the adjustment problem would be solved.)

A second British reservation concerned Commonwealth trade and financial arrangements. Lord Beaverbrook wrote me a rather angry letter after the first edition of *Sterling-Dollar Diplomacy*, saying: 'You may have the idea that my opposition ... was contentious or obscurantist. It was, as I see it, the attitude of one who sought to reconcile his belief in the Empire with his hope that a strong Empire was the best ally the United States could have. Was I wrong?' Well, of course, he was. Empire was not a viable economic or political concept for Britain after World War II. It took a long time for some members of the British public and political leadership to recognize that fact. Keynes scathingly denounced such members of the House of Commons as wanting to 'build up a separate economic bloc which excludes Canada and consists of countries to which we already owe more than we can pay, on the basis of their agreeing to lend us money they have not got and buy only from us and one another goods we are unable to supply.' Yet despite Keynes' eloquence, there remained a lingering commitment to the sterling area and preference. Part of the explanation was the failure to recognize the full and terrible weight of the war on Britain, to realize that the postwar situation would be radically different and that Britain could no longer run a reserve currency. Perhaps there was also the feeling that the sterling balances and the preferences would be useful things to have because they might guarantee Britain assured exports in the postwar period. On the part of some there was also the desire to maintain Commonwealth economic and financial ties as a means of maintaining Commonwealth political relationships.

Perhaps most important of all there was in Britain no less than in the United States an 'arrogance of economic power.' Neither country, when it came down to it, wanted to surrender its reserve currency status and throw itself unreservedly into an international financial arrangement. If that statement was not true for Keynes himself, it certainly applied to the people in the Bank of England and others in London with whom Keynes had to deal and whose acquiescence was required for a Bretton Woods settlement.

In hindsight, we may say that the reluctance of the United Kingdom to surrender or share its reserve currency role has been one of the major causes of its postwar difficulties. During the wartime negotiations us officials suggested the possibility of a multilateral effort to scale down and fund the sterling balances (the funding was to be through the IMF). Admittedly, the suggestion was hardly more than a hint, but history might have been very different — and very much better for both sides — if the hint had been picked up. Of course, a scaling down and funding of the balances would have been politically possible only if the United States had been willing to offer a big chunk of direct aid to holders of the balances like India, Pakistan, and Egypt. It is possible that the American negotiators were not prepared to face up to the full implications of a genuine solution to the sterling problem.

Let us now try to draw these threads together. How, in summary, did the intellectual, economic, and political forces on both sides of the Atlantic affect the final outcome at Bretton Woods? In what major respects does the Bretton Woods compromise need revision today? In answering these questions I would focus on four main points:

First, the emphasis on universal organization on both sides of the Atlantic led to the neglect of regional arrangements, a neglect that had to be corrected later, beginning with the Marshall Plan. We are still struggling with the question of how regional arrangements can be accommodated to the universal design.

Second, there was an underestimate on both sides of the magnitude of the liquidity problem. Neither side foresaw that inflation would double the price of commodities over the prewar level and that the stock of gold would be inadequate to finance world trade and payments. Nobody foresaw the extent to which new gold production would be discouraged by the concurrence of inflation with a fixed gold price. The liquidity problem was not understood in the same way that we understand it today.

The lack of foresight was particularly striking, of course, on the American side. The US negotiators were worried about Congress; they could not take for granted that even the modest White plan would be accepted. They fought the overdraft concept of the Clearing Union, pressed for a depository scheme in which drawing rights were strictly related to contributions, insisted on conditional rather than unconditional liquidity and smaller quotas for countries like France than those countries wanted. All of these policies worked against US interests and had to be reversed by American negotiators two decades later.

If the United States had accepted the Keynes plan in its original form and had undertaken postwar aid to Europe through the Clearing Union rather than through Marshall Aid, the US would have accumulated over $30 billion of overdraft facilities which would have financed nearly all of the US deficits in the 1950s and the 1960s. Admittedly, too much should not be made of that point. The Keynes plan would not have been the right device for postwar reconstruction. Still, it would have served the long-term US interest to have negotiated on the basis of the Keynes plan, adapting it as necessary to remove its inflationary bias and its other defects. Fortunately, this failure has been remedied a quarter of a century later by the activation of the facility for Special Drawing Rights in the International Monetary Fund. At long last we have achieved what Keynes wanted — a quantum of international reserves automatically available to all countries that can be increased in accordance with the needs of world trade. However, we still have to solve the problem of assuring the orderly coexistence of different reserve assets — gold, dollars, sterling, and SDRs.

Third, the interaction of American and British forces left us with no adequate solution to the adjustment problem. In a way this is curious, because the first drafts of the White and Keynes plans did deal boldly with this issue. In their original form, the American and British currency plans faced the adjustment issue squarely — they provided for far-reaching international control over the economic policies of deficit and surplus countries. Under the first (unpublished) draft of the White plan, members were obliged 'not to adopt any monetary or banking measure promoting either serious inflation or serious deflation without the consent of a majority of members' votes of the Fund.' The published version omitted this far-reaching (and politically unrealistic) provision, but authorized the Fund to make recommendations for changes in the economic policy of countries going too far toward deficit or surplus. Moreover, recommendations could be reinforced by sanctions — the denial of the use of Fund resources beyond a certain point for a deficit country, the rationing of the 'scarce currency' in the case of a country in surplus. Under the Keynes plan, the Clearing Union could *require* a deficit country that drew more than one-half of its overdraft facilities to deposit collateral, depreciate its currency, control outward capital movements, or surrender liquid reserves in reduction of its debit balance. It could recommend to that country internal economic measures needed to restore equilibrium. It could *require* a surplus country whose credit balance exceeded half its quota to carry out such measures as the stimulation of domestic demand, the appreciation of its currency, the reduction of import barriers, and the making of international development loans.

With the notable exception of the 'scarce currency' clause, most of these references to international supervision of the economic policies of deficit and surplus countries were eliminated during negotiation of the Fund articles. In part this was owing to differences between the United States and Britain on the relative emphasis to be accorded to deficit and surplus country responsibilities; it was also because of the fact that explicit qualifications of economic sovereignty would alienate congressional and parliamentary opinion. Thus the Bretton Woods compromise left a good deal of ambiguity about the responsibilities for adjustment of surplus and deficit countries. It ruled out adjustment through freely fluctuating exchange rates or by controls on payments for current transactions — since exchange stability and multilateral trade were two primary Bretton Woods objectives. But it said very little about how adjustment *was* to be achieved. The architects at Bretton Woods apparently hoped that, with the aid of Fund resources, deficit and surplus countries could be relied on to restore a balance within a relatively short time by reasonable domestic policies and by occasional changes in exchange rates to correct a 'fundamental disequilibrium.' Unfortunately, however, this system just has not worked out.

The inadequacies of the Bretton Woods adjustment mechanism were camouflaged in the early postwar years when the United States was in surplus and the rest of the world was in deficit. Nobody paid much attention to the problem of how the Fund would 'police' surplus and deficit nations to assure their good behaviour. In effect, the United States 'policed' itself – adopting liberal aid and trade policies appropriate to a surplus nation because it quickly recognized that if it failed to do so the rest of the world would go broke. This was not a question of American altruism, but rather of enlightened self-interest.

The United States was the economic giant among nations; there was no one with whom to share responsibility; it alone had the power to save the wartime multilateral dream and assure the survival of freedom in the West. The political costs of failure were unacceptable to it and, consequently, it was willing to pay the price in the Marshall Plan, other measures of postwar aid, and unrequited tariff cuts. Nobody had to invoke the principal Fund sanction envisaged for 'policing' the creditor – the 'scarce currency' clause considered so important by Keynes. It was unavailable, in any case, since the Fund was inactive during the period of US reconstruction aid and dollars in the Fund were not technically 'scarce.' But for the reasons mentioned above it was not needed.

When 'dollar shortage' gave way to 'dollar glut' and a US-centred system was replaced by a more balanced distribution of economic power, the shortcomings in the Bretton Woods design became apparent. The countries of continental Europe did not 'police' themselves in the direction of creditor-country responsibility following the earlier American model. It was not that they were more 'wicked' than than the United States; but because none of them was big enough to be decisive, they did not assume the same responsibility the United States had done for 'saving the system.' The French used growing gold reserves to support an independent economic and political role, with little heed to co-operation through the Fund. (France unwillingly had to disgorge half of its $6 billion gold stock after the May 1968 disorders, but student rioters such as Cohn-Bendit can hardly be considered part of the permanent adjustment mechanism!) The Germans were equally reluctant to accept the Fund's concept of creditor-country responsibility.

As they face the 1970s, therefore, the United States, Britain, Canada, and other countries are still struggling with the difficult adjustment issue they confronted at Bretton Woods a quarter of a century ago. The United States is seeking to improve its payments position by a total of about $10 billion a year. Which are the countries prepared to see their payments positions reduced by this amount (or even by this amount minus allocations of SDRs)? And, quite apart from the specific American payments problem, just what methods of adjustment are countries agreed to use? Are they to place primary reliance on trade and capital controls, on fluctuating exchange rates, or on the harmonization of domestic and foreign economic policies? Until greater progress is made in resolving these questions, we are likely to stumble from crisis to crisis.

One way to improve the international adjustment process would be to give international agencies the kind of influence over the economic policies of deficit and surplus countries that was envisaged in the original US and British currency plans. For example, there could be more regular and systematic consultation among senior government officials so that international adjustment is given greater weight in national policy-making. More progress could also be made in the adjustment of national policies on military spending, foreign aid, and private capital flows to help reduce imbalances of payments.

In the years immediately ahead, however, it is unlikely that the adjustment problem will be fully resolved by measures of this kind. Economic sovereignty dies hard. Deficit and surplus countries are reluctant to sacrifice domestic economic objectives for the purpose of external balance; even when prepared to do so they do not always have the policy instruments available to get sufficiently quick results. And there are limits to their willingness to adjust foreign spending in the interest of payments balance.

For these reasons, it is encouraging that the international community is taking a new look at the possibilities of easing the adjustment problem through greater flexibility in exchange rates. The present adjustable peg system of the IMF permits changes to take place, but only after the political leaders of a country find them necessary to cure a 'fundamental disequilibrium.' For reasons of prestige or domesitc politics, national leaders are frequently reluctant to devalue or revalue a currency; as in the case of the pound sterling and the mark, they tend to postpone changes too long and to make them only after a currency crisis has developed.

Like many others, I believe the best way to provide for greater flexibility in exchange rates is through the 'crawling peg,' under which a currency could move up or down one or two percentage points a year through a series of tiny changes every week or so. The changes would take place in response to a formula designed to move the rate in the direction necessary to restore balance, thus taking the responsibility off the shoulders of the political leaders. In addition, we should permit exchange rates to fluctuate within a 'wider band' (such as the 2¼ per cent on either side of parity agreed to at the end of 1971).

Although some have argued that greater exchange flexibility will unsettle the confidence of international traders and investors, a modest combination of crawling peg and wider band should commend itself to the financial community as a desirable substitute for the present arrangement. After all, a substantial risk of a very small rate change may be preferable to the small (but far from negligible) possibility of a very substantial rate change that exists at present, particularly if the new system makes exchange and trade restrictions less likely and eases the adjustment problem of a troubled world economy.

My fourth and final observation has to do with our international arrangements for monetary decision-making. It was envisaged at Bretton Woods by both the US and Britain as well as everybody else that the International Monetary Fund would be the central place for taking decisions on the liquidity and adjustment problems. It has not worked out that way, for several reasons. One, I believe, was the decision, taken at the Savannah Conference two years after Bretton Woods at the insistence of Fred Vinson, the US secretary of the Treasury, to have full-time executive directors. As a result of this decision, we have a rather inadequate system for managing our international monetary affairs. There are the annual meetings of the Fund in which the responsible decision-makers get together for a week, and they pass a lot of resolutions; but with more than one hundred countries represented, the amount of real business that can be done is limited. And these meetings are only once a year. The rest of the time you have the executive directors permanently resident in Washington and, meaning no disrespect to them, they are not the people with responsibility for making the real decisions in capitals. This has left a serious gap.

In recent years we have developed a parallel structure for decision-making on liquidity and adjustment problems outside the Fund – the Group of Ten, the Basle Club, and the OECD. This has meant a diffusion of responsibility among a number of forums for monetary policy-making. Moreover, these new forums are all 'rich men's clubs,' the less-developed countries are excluded from decision-making on very important matters. They resent this – and with some justice. Countries like India and Brazil have an important stake in how these questions are resolved – on how much liquidity is created, on how adjustment is to take place. The way these matters are resolved affects the amount of foreign aid the less-developed countries get and the extent to which they will have a chance to sell their exports in the markets of the developed world.

One way to correct this situation would be to create a Group of Twenty-One consisting of the countries with nationals on the executive board of the Fund, plus Switzerland. They could meet at the ministerial level every three months, alternately at the headquarters of the Fund and at the Fund office in Paris or at other places. This consultative Group of Twenty-One operating at the ministerial level would provide the element we now lack – a mechanism for the continuous high-level discussion of international financial problems with the participation of key countries from the Third World.

Ansel Luxford, the chief Treasury lawyer in the American delegation at Bretton Woods, sent me a letter some years ago containing a good deal of wisdom. It may be appropriate to quote part of it today:

To me, then as now, the major significance of Bretton Woods was the death blow it represented in victory over the economic isolationism of the prewar period and the serious threat that with military victory this country would again revert to economic nationalism. Thus, the question of how effective the Bank and Fund may have been in the light of postwar events (many of them not foreseeable except by hindsight) is not nearly so important as having established the principle of US cooperation in the solution of the international economic problems of the future.

Let me admit that Bretton Woods' sails had to be trimmed to the point where public and Congressional acceptance might be possible – but only then after a life and death fight. Let me admit that the package was wrapped in the glittering generalities of a hard political fight designed to get public acceptance and force Congressional approval. My answer is that both courses in my opinion were essential to establishing the major principle and are entirely in harmony with what we all know to be the realities of mobilizing political action in this country.

Having established the principle and having obtained public acceptance thereof, the ground was paved for the British Loan, Marshall Aid, etc. To my way of thinking, the basic differences between the British and US approaches were not matters of economic theory or even disagreements over the major economic factors involved. The real question was how to equate economic principle with the realities of both British and US political life (to say nothing of the other interested countries).

I believe this historical judgment will be convincing to anyone who understands the conditions in which the Bretton Woods negotiations took place. We can criticize the negotiators for excessive preoccupation with economics, but surely we are fortunate that they used the occasion of World War II to create the economic institutions that made our extraordinary postwar recovery possible. Had there been no Bretton Woods Conference during World War II, it might not have been possible to negotiate a Fund or Bank at all; the solidarity and idealism of the war would have been dissipated. We can criticize the postwar planners, too, for unrealistic universalist dreams. But surely we are fortunate that they established universal institutions linking the developed countries of the West to the developing countries and potentially to the countries of Eastern Europe.

'There is,' Keynes warned at Savannah, 'scarcely any enduringly successful experience of an international body which has fulfilled the hopes of its progenitors. Either an institution has become diverted to the instrument of a limited group, or it has been a puppet of sawdust through which the breath of life does not blow.' One cannot escape the conclusion that Keynes, perfectionist though he was, would have been the first to acknowledge the service to the general interest and the continuing vitality of the institutions in whose conception he played such a decisive part.

Louis Rasminsky
William A. Mackintosh
A.F.W. Plumptre
John J. Deutsch

CANADIAN VIEWS

LOUIS RASMINSKY

In the years preceding Bretton Woods, in spite of the very pressing preoccupations that we had, we began to turn our thoughts to the sort of monetary system we wanted to have after the war. So far as I was concerned, the high spot intellectually in the discussions that preceded Bretton Woods was reached at the meetings held in London in 1942 to discuss the Clearing Union proposal. We were worried in Canada about the shape that British economic policy would take after war. We knew that a very influential force in determining that shape would be Keynes. Without much warning, in the spring of 1942, we were confronted with the Clearing Union paper which put the influence of Keynes clearly on the side of multilateralism in which we, of course, on account of our position between Britain and the United States and on account of the structure of our balance of payments, had a very great interest. Keynes was excited by the concept of the Clearing Union. At the discussions he was accompanied by people of similar intellectual stature, like Lionel Robbins. Keynes was very open-minded, and he approached the Clearing Union idea as one that was open for discussion and not as something where he was quite sure that the British were right. I think it would be very difficult to overestimate the importance of the conversion of Keynes to multilateralism. The forces operating on the other side were very strong. If Keynes had not come down on the side of multilateralism we might have had quite a different situation after the war.

We were attracted in Canada by the beauty of the concept of the Clearing

Union plan, by the overdraft principle which made it so clear that the sum of the debits had to equal the sum of the credits. But we were worried even before we went to London about the acceptability of the plan to the American Congress because the US was the only substantial creditor in sight. Our apprehensions on this score were enhanced by the virtually unlimited extent of the commitment requested of creditor countries. Also, as the discussion proceeded, there was the question of stabilization of primary product prices in which Lionel Robbins played a leading part. There was the question of postwar relief. There was a recognition that there was a problem of international investment and international trade. We found that there was some tendency to feel that the Clearing Union could do everything; and of course on the assumption that the creditor does not care how much money he puts up in this way the Clearing Union could have done everything. We were concerned that relief would give rise to indebtedness under the Clearing Union scheme which we did not think was right. We were concerned that if the Clearing Union were used to finance primary product stabilization schemes it would look as though the whole thing was done with mirrors and any inhibitions on the fixing of prices would be removed. So we came to the conclusion reluctantly that the Clearing Union concept was not a starter.

I recall one instance in the London discussions which enhanced our concern about the virtually unlimited extent of the commitment on creditors. A senior official of the British Treasury, when we raised the question as to whether creditor countries would be willing to accept all the bancor that they could accumulate by the drawings of the debtor countries, said that any creditor country that accumulates a credit balance in bancor to the extent of this quota should be expelled from the union. One of the Australians, not to be outdone, said that any debtor country who accumulated a debit balance with the union to the extent of his quota should have his debit balance forgiven.

In these discussions the dominating factor in Keynes' mind was the emphasis on the need to maintain full employment after the war and this explains the size of the quotas that he proposed. It explains also the emphasis that he placed, which he moved away from later, on the facility with which countries could change their exchange rates. In some of the original published versions of the Clearing Union plan there was a provision that the country could use 25 per cent of its quota and continue depreciating its currency by 5 per cent year after year. After these discussions that was changed to a possible 5 per cent once-and-for-all depreciation after two years.

In the White-Bernstein plan there was a good deal more emphasis originally on the supranational character of the Fund. The original concept was that the Fund could fix the initial exchange rates and the Fund could require countries to change their exchange rates. In this earlier version the Fund would have much more influence on domestic policy than anything that was provided in the later plan. Probably the consideration of what Congress would put up with explains why there was a movement away from this emphasis on the Fund as an active directing organization in the later American versions of the plan. Having in mind the *real* distribution of economic power at the time, my overall impression is that the Americans moved a very great distance, that they did not exploit that power in determining the final version at Bretton Woods. They went a very great distance towards meeting the British view. I would naturally like to think that Canadians played some part in that. I do not honestly know whether we did or not. We came to the conclusion in the spring of 1943 that we should have a shot at it and we produced a proposal, the details of which I will not cover here.

We adopted the American form of a 'mixed bag of currencies' but we provided for a larger fund. The small size of the originally proposed American fund was quite consistent with the concept of an activist fund; not much extra liquidity would be needed. We provided for a larger fund and we introduced for the first time in these discussions the concept of the right of the Fund to borrow from particular members, which ultimately became the underlying concept of the GAB arrangement. We provided for a bit more flexibility with regard to changes in exchange rates than in the American proposals and we objected to the extent of the veto power that the Americans were originally asking over major decisions. We left only a veto on a change in the price of gold. We provided for virtually immediate withdrawal from the Fund on the part of a country that wished to leave, a proposal that was designed to deal with the problem of an attack on the basis of loss of sovereignty which we anticipated would come up in national legislatures.

Looking back, it seems to me that the problem that Bretton Woods sought to deal with was the right problem, namely how to reconcile the desire for high employment with the avoidance of external policies of a destructive sort. This problem reflected the concern to avoid a repetition of a major depression, as there was a widespread belief during the war that, as most wars have in the past, this war would be followed by a severe depression; and, secondly, the desire to avoid a repetition of the nationalistic international trade and exchange practices and the unco-ordinated exchange rate fluctuations of the 1930s. I am prepared to express dogmatically the opinion that by and large the Bretton Woods system has worked. However, since the end of the war we have had one of the great periods of world economic expansion. We have had almost continual economic progress in terms of growth of real output, accompanied by a reduction in trade barriers and an increase in the amount of trade which has been even greater than the increase in real output. So, without denying that there have been and are very serious problems, I say that the system has worked. In fact, I think I would go further than that and say that I believe the Fund has come as close, up to the present, to achieving its objectives as any international organization that was created after the war. Bretton Woods addressed itself to the real problems, and basically the decisions that were taken pointed us in the right direction.

One of the results of the establishment of the Fund that has not received enough emphasis is the great increase in international consultation and collaboration. This seems so obvious that it may seem jejune even to mention it, but to those of us who saw what international co-operation in these matters was before the war the difference is dramatic. For a person like myself, for example, who worked at the League of Nations from 1930 to 1939 on the economic side of things and as the secretary of the Financial Committee, the difference in the amount and the character of consultation is spectacular. Before the war, there was great diffidence about discussing anybody's domestic economic policies or the impact of those policies on other countries' positions, and discussions tended to be focused exclusively on 'external' economic policy such as tariff barriers. Such external manifestations provided the main theme of the 1933 World Economic Conference. If one contrasts that with the frequency and intimacy of the discussions which now take place on the board of the Fund and in other forums one becomes aware of a very major achievement.

The Fund set up codes of behaviour with regard to exchange matters which essentially I think are still valid. The code of behaviour mainly consists of two things: one is the recognition that exchange rates are properly matters of international concern; that the exchange rate of country A on country B is also the exchange rate of country B on country A and that some technique is needed for agreeing to exchange rates and for agreeing to change exchange rates. The second part of the code was the decision to do away with exchange restrictions on current accounts. To achieve its objectives and help in the reconciliation of full employment and external balance, the Fund established financing facilities. With the benefit of hindsight it is clear that we did not look at the liquidity problem quite in the same way as we do now. We tended to think of the facilities more as responsive to balance-of-payments deficits that countries might incur rather than as introducing a growth factor. The amounts set up originally were small. The quotas have been increased twice, first by 50 per cent and later by 25 per cent. They have been enlarged by the GAB arrangement. There have been other facilities through central bank credits. This process has been inevitably one of evolution and with SDRs, I hope in the bag, there is no reason for feeling that evolution has come to an end. All these steps are more and more in the direction of having the Fund act like a central bank, as a creator of liquidity. Of course in that context SDRs are a major step forward, because it does give power to the managing director and the board to make a decision regarding the creation of liquidity.

At the same time as it provided financing facilities, the Fund agreement set up certain techniques or pressures towards equilibrium. In the nature of things, the pressures on debtor countries are stronger in the real world than the pressures on creditor countries. You can run out of foreign exchange; you cannot really run out of your own currency. But it was a remarkable step forward that the Americans recognized the responsibility of creditor countries in the 'scarce currency' provision. In a way the 'scarce currency' provision *was* put into effect through the EPU system which constituted an organized and accepted discrimination against the United States dollar on the part of the European countries. That system came to an end when the dollar shortage came to an end. It is an interesting question why no one proposed that the 'scarce currency' provision be put into effect in the case of Germany. I suppose that the answer lies in the feeling that the reduction in trade barriers which we were able to achieve is too fragile a thing, too uncertain, to warrant running the major risk that would be run if you had organized exchange discrimination against Germany. Perhaps other people on the panel will have other ideas.

You may think I have spoken pretty complacently about Bretton Woods. I would certainly be far from claiming that there was perfect foresight and that the instrument is perfect. One can play the game of asking what would be done differently if one had the chance. There are a number of things quite clearly we did not foresee. We did not foresee the extent to which inflation would be a problem after the war. We had our eyes fixed on the opposite danger. We did not foresee the extent to which exchange controls would be abolished after the war. The articles of agreement of the Fund are friendly to the idea of exchange control. It was practically assumed that there will be exchange controls on capital, and the Fund can in fact require countries in certain circumstances to impose exchange controls rather than use the resources of the Fund to finance capital transfers. The movement towards convertibility went perhaps further than most of us thought that it would. At the same time, the amount of liquidity in the world increased more than we had thought it would, both national liquidity and more recently international liquidity in the form, for example, of Euro-dollar deposits. We did not foresee the reluctance that governments would have to adjust the adjustable peg. This reluctance, which I suppose is normally politically motivated, may be connected with the liquidity increase that I just mentioned. There has been more scope for, and more of, short-term international capital movements of a precautionary or of a speculatory source. Governments have in the attempt to allay them made public statements about their unwillingness, or their lack of any intention, to change the exchange rate and have found themselves in a sense hoist on that petard. It may be that the reluctance to depreciate exchange rates is also a reflection of the inflationary situation that has been so prevalent and the fear that the increased cost of imports would aggravate domestic inflationary tendencies. These are things that we did not foresee at Bretton Woods, and I suppose that if one had it to do over again one would look for some sort of mechanism that would prevent speculation – or rather which would increase the risks attached to speculation. At the present time there is often only one direction in which exchange rates can be moved. At the same time I think one would want to be cautious about adopting techniques that will discourage governments and central banks from dealing with inflationary problems that have been so general.

There is one final thing that I would like to comment on and that is the way the Fund is set up. This has been, as the Managing Director knows, a favourite theme of mine for some years. I believe that a serious mistake was made in setting the Fund up on a basis which has now resulted in all the executive directors of the Fund being full-time resident directors. We fought this battle alongside the British at Savannah and were instrumental in getting the compromise that made it possible for there to be a part-time director provided he had a full-time alternate. I operated on that basis for many years and so did Otmar Emminger when Germany first came into the Fund. The difficulty connected with the other system is precisely the one that Professor Gardner has described. The executive directors of the Fund are very able people, but it seems to me that what one wants, if the Fund is to play the leading role in policy determination, is the participation of people who play some part themselves in determining national policy; you don't get that in the Fund right now. There are problems here, particularly in the case of directors that represent a good many countries. But, I hope in some way or other, the diffusion of authority that has taken place, with a good deal of the authority being transferred to the G 10 or to WP 3 or to Basle, can be re-versed. To the extent that this proves possible, the Fund will be able to play a more policy-initiating role (rather than a responsive role) than it has been possible for it to do over the past ten or fifteen years.

W.A. MACKINTOSH

My relationship with discussions on the postwar international financial system started in 1942. I found the Clearing Union proposal presented by Keynes to be fascinating. However, I was always bothered by what seemed to me an unresolved contradiction. Keynes, as I recall, argued that his idea in-troduced into the international sphere the concept of bank expansion as it takes place in the national sphere. He asserted forcefully that the member countries of the Clearing Union should draw on it as of right and not as peti-tioners. This view did not fit the other features of his plan which called for an organization which was governed not by a board of trustees *in absentia* but by a very strong management which would decide whether to put bancor into buffer stocks, into relief, or into international investments, to name some of the things that were suggested. This aspect involved discrimination. That the solution found at Bretton Woods was the right one I would not assert, but some compromise was necessary.

Another impression I retained was the difficulty one had with both the British belief in the permanence of the US surplus and the Americans' theo-logical involvements in the iniquity of the British preferences (Mr Gardner, I think, called them fixations; I usually called them theological convictions). The British had also some fixation on the subject of full employment. But the spokesmen who had absolute ideas about full employment were the Australians. I recall a discussion when the Australians proposed that within an international agreement there should be additional clauses requiring coun-tries, as a condition and subject to ferocious penalties, to maintain full em-ployment. Keynes murmured 'Be good, sweet maid, and *very* clever.'

There were many points in the International Monetary Agreement at which the Canadians, particularly Mr Rasminsky, made important and clarifying contributions. In successive preliminary discussions we probably had considerable effect in converting the British to a multilateral approach despite the persistent efforts of Sir Hubert Henderson and Mr Thomas Balogh. On the views of United States officials concerning the British preference we had at least an eroding effect, so that preferential tariffs became subjects for negotiation and not illegal weapons to be given up at the door.

A.F.W. PLUMPTRE

My different point of view lies in the fact that I was not a participant in the preparatory discussions prior to Bretton Woods, but I was in Washington representing the Canadian government; and while I did have some association with the US Treasury, with people like Mr Bernstein and others, my primary job lay with the wartime agencies in Washington, representing a Canadian wartime agency with the US War Production Board, with the Office of Price Administration, and to some extent with the State Department. It seems to me that I might add to this session by giving my own personal picture of wartime Washington, leading up to Bretton Woods, which is a little different from Professor Gardner's presentation and incidentally diverges somewhat from Sir Roy Harrod's overtones vis-à-vis the United States.

I think there are three points I would like to talk about very briefly; one is domestic politics in the United States with special reference to the New Deal; the second is the peculiarities of the Roosevelt cabinet system; and third is the point that Bretton Woods was an ABC affair, America, Britain, and Canada, and that made it in some sense unique.

First of all, about the New Deal. Going to Washington, as I did some years before Bretton Woods, I immediately became enormously impressed by the great political gulf between the left-wing New Dealers and the right-wing business people. The War Production Board was essentially a businessman's organization, but the OPA, which at that time was the monopoly of people like Leon Henderson, Kenneth Galbraith, and other types of that sort, belonged to the left-wing New Deal. Certain persons in the Treasury, Harry White outstanding and Frank Coe, an ex-associate of mine at the University of Toronto, again were very much left-wing 'New Deal' in their thinking. Other people in the Treasury were of quite a different background and frame of mind, and in the White House staff itself there was a wide spectrum of opinion: some like Laughlin Currie were very close to Harry White, and there were others with a quite dissimilar approach to politics and to economics.

I think it is difficult to appreciate Washington in those days without reminding oneself of the appalling depths of the depression of the 1930s in the United States and of the fact that the New Deal itself represented, if not a revolution, a near-revolution in American politics. Whatever it may have been in other countries it was not, for the United States, just another slump; it was a traumatic experience which led to different attitudes amongst different people, and in Washington, as I found it, the left-wing New Dealers whom I have mentioned were anti-establishment with a passion and a zeal and often with a venom which is difficult even to recall in retrospect. (This, incidentally, had its backlash when Eisenhower came to power and we had the McCarthy episodes as a violent reaction against the infiltration of 'communism' into the American government.)

The decisions about the executive directors of the Fund and Bank, what sort of people they were to be and where they were to be located, is in my mind an outcome of the vigorous and violent antipathy to Wall Street and New York which exited in New Deal Washington. This, of course, came to a head in the excoriation of the money-changers of Wall Street in the Pecora Hearings and in the revelations of all sorts of 'goings on' of Wall Street which came out in the mid-thirties. The idea of permanent executive directors in general impinges on the particular part played by Harry White. I think Secretary Vinson came to believe (but I think it was more Harry White's view than Vinson's) that this was necessary. In my opinion one cannot understand this sort of pressure without reference to this background.

I think one would also have to ask the question whether in fact the Fund would have worked better if it had not been located in Washington and if the dominant influence on it had been, let us say, the Federal Reserve Bank of New York as contrasted with the Treasury at Washington. A quite different sort of thing might have emerged. I myself am a wild radical at heart and my sympathies were with the New Dealers with whom I happened to be working.

Turning to influences on world trade and investment, not only were the goings on of Wall Street affecting in a very serious manner the internal financial structure of the United States but they, of course, affected its external finance. The goings on of Wall Street financial houses were in no area more flagrantly anti-social than in their selling of Latin American bonds in the latter stages of the 1920s. The SEC was, of course, domestically a partial response to these goings on. But a further response was a feeling by the New

Dealers that international finance, particularly the export of capital by the United States, had to be controlled through a responsible agency in Washington, and could not be left to the vagaries of the private bankers. A world bank located in Washington would channel to the world outside a more stable flow of international capital than had been visible from the United States during the 1920s and 1930s.

Now a word or two about the Roosevelt concept of a cabinet. In regard to his cabinet he was notoriously *laissez-faire*, allowing his various cabinet members to go their various ways. It always seemed to me that, perhaps luckily this is reflected in the world organization that emerged after the war. Professor Gardner has spoken of a unitary organization; but one of the great features of the United Nations and its specialized agencies is its non-unitarianism. You have a great variety of organizations, and in my mind this responded to the variety and independence of the agencies of wartime Washington. The world of the future was not to have just a League of Nations, at which the State Department would be represented, but it would have a whole complex of organizations in which each of the Washington departments would have 'its own' international agency. One had a proliferation of agencies, and my own feeling is that this has been for the general good of the world because it has enlarged the involvement of persons in all sorts of departments of all sorts of governments.

Accordingly, I do not regard what happened in Bretton Woods as simply the result of a split between State and Treasury departments or between Hull and Morgenthau; the fact of the matter was that many departments of government in the United States were getting their own specialized agencies, not just the Treasury getting its own Bretton Woods against the opposition of the State Department. The economic side of the State Department did get a bit of an agency, quite apart from the UN itself, in the GATT and this represented the economic objective closest to Cordell Hull's own heart — that is to say, progress towards free trade or freer trade. They did not get the International Trade Organization which, of course, would have involved a lot of other US departments (the Department of Commerce, the Department of Justice, and so forth). But other agencies came into being — the Labor Department already had its own agency, as also did Agriculture. So I do not think one should regard Bretton Woods as an isolated instance. It was part of what I regard as a highly desirable and decentralized postwar pattern.

One of the great contributions of this decentralization was that the different international bodies could have different forms of self-government.

An unmentioned achievement of Bretton Woods was that a structure, an accepted structure, of international government was created which did not give each country one vote. A system of government was accepted with weighted voting and this allowed things to happen in quite a different way from the way they would have happened in a unitary system with one country, one vote.

One result is that there is now a group of twenty directors, most of them representing a variety of countries. Time has run against the possibility of having executive directors still actively engaged in senior positions in their own countries. Most of the executive directors now represent several countries, some of them up to a score of countries. To have one man supposedly speaking for all but living in one capital of the twenty and commuting to Washington is not very viable. I think this is a real problem with the Fund and Bank. My own question is not whether the objective we were seeking was right, but I question that it is achievable, given the non-resident executive directors system.

Finally, the question about Bretton Woods being an ABC affair. It was in large measure an American, British, and Canadian affair, but so were a lot of other things in Washington until the end of hostilities, until the French and other European governments became more than exile governments. Washington, indeed, was a surprisingly ABC affair during the war. The Chiefs of Staff were the combined chiefs of staff of the US and the UK, but the Canadians had a large and influential mission attached to them. The Combined Production and Resources Board was an ABC board; the Combined Food Board was an ABC board; the Combined Raw Materials Board was only an AB board, simply because C, Canada, would not go in (C.D. Howe felt we would have more leverage from the outside than by being voted down on the inside). So the international agencies, particularly those that were formed before the end of hostilities, naturally had this sort of cast. It may well be that the team which Canada fielded in the Bretton Woods areas was a particularly good one, and this, as Sir Roy Harrod said in his biography of Lord Keynes, played an important part. But I think that one of our concerns, in looking at the Fund and Bank, is to realize that they still contain certain overtones of that original ABC cast. I certainly feel that, had Bretton Woods come a little later, the European countries would have been more integrally involved in the formulation of the Fund and the subsequent activities than, from time to time, they have been.

Another ABC type of thinking which I think is significant particularly concerns the World Bank. The International Development Association is, to my mind, very largely a North American concept. It has strong overtones of a 'Community Chest.' Everybody is expected to put something up, and you have a 'contributions committee' which goes around and puts the finger on the people who have not put up what they should have in relation to all the public statistics and so forth. But the fact of the matter is, as I discovered, on that darkened continent called Europe they don't have community chests, and therefore the whole concept does not really ring a bell, at least not the same sort of peremptory bell as in North America.

J.J. DEUTSCH

I had the privilege as a junior officer in the Department of External Affairs of participating both in the preparatory work leading to Bretton Woods and the other international organizations, and also to be present at Bretton Woods itself as a junior member of the delegation. Among the greatest concerns that we had were two highly unfavourable possibilities with regard to postwar developments: the prospect of the continuing inconvertibility of sterling and economic isolationism by the United States.

These were the things that Canadians were very much preoccupied with at that time. The depression had struck Canada hard, particularly through international channels by the breakdown of the international exchanges and the Smoot-Hawley tariff in the US. We were terribly concerned that Canada might be facing this kind of world in the postwar period. Consequently, the initiatives which were undertaken in the State Department, looking toward a universal multilateral approach to world trade problems and the idea of some kind of international organization that would bring about better order in the international exchanges and the restoration of convertible currencies in the postwar period, were greatly welcomed in Canada. As these were very attractive prospects for Canada, we decided we would encourage both these initiatives and back them strongly.

We soon found that in our dealings with the United States there were two quite distinct but related groups, the financial group in the Treasury and the trade group in the State Department. Elsewhere there was another body that was very important to us in those days, the United States Department of Agriculture. It was something of an ogre which, it seemed to us, was trying to stop all progress. The agricultural interests would do anything to protect agricultural prices, or to reserve their domestic markets for agricultural products. They would readily accept inconvertibility of sterling if that was the way to sell their goods, or a protectionist policy if that was the best way to protect agriculture. However, in this situation the Canadians did play, I think, a significant part in trying to keep matters moving on both fronts. On both the financial and the trade front Canadians often served as ambassadors between the State Department and the Treasury during many a meeting. Indeed, Canadians always insisted that adherence to the Bretton Woods programme would depend upon progress being made on the trade front on a multilateral basis. I think this was actually put forward as a condition of Canadian adherence as part of our attempt to hold these things together and to keep them moving in parallel.

Frankly, at the time we were very much concerned that the trade programme would not be feasible. We were fairly sceptical that the British would really move very far in the direction of trade liberalization. We found that there were two very strong schools of thought on the British side. It was never clear which side was going to prevail. From one side there was concerted pressure on Canada during the early postwar years to go along with a regional concept involving the continued inconvertibility of sterling and a British Commonwealth system of trade. Even after the Bretton Woods agreements were implemented, this pressure was continued. I remember coming back from Geneva immediately after the negotiations to establish the GATT, at a time when we were having exchange difficulties, and learning that the Canadian Prime Minister had just received a letter from the British Prime Minister inviting us to join the sterling area. In this invitation a programme was laid out designed to help us with our difficulties, and also to provide a future for us.

We were then in difficulties owing to a loss of exchange reserves, because we had over-lent to finance exports. We had lent at too fast a rate, and we ran down our reserves to the point of danger. We faced the necessity of imposing import restrictions. There was an irony about this because we had taken the lead in getting a system which would result in the abolition of quantitative restrictions in world trade. Indeed, we pressed this extremely hard because the US Treasury was inclined rather to accept trade restrictions but not exchange restrictions. The latter were evil, but trade restrictions were all right if that were necessary. But now we found ourselves having to impose trade restrictions in order to protect our exchange reserves. Then came this strong invitation from the British to reconsider our whole posture and come into the sterling area, and to become part of a sterling system of trade. It fell to my lot to prepare the draft of a letter to the British Prime Minister firmly turning down this proposition. This incident is an indication of the persistence with which this particular approach was pursued by one side in Britain. The Canadian position was based on strong doubts that the British could really reconstruct and maintain this sterling system, and on the conviction that the multilateral approach of the Bretton Woods agreements was more in the Canadian interest.

In the outcome I share the optimism and the positive view of what Bretton Woods has accomplished. Indeed, we achieved convertibility of currencies at a much earlier period than I would have thought possible, and in a much more extensive way than I would have thought feasible. Similarly, the end of the economic isolation of the United States was accomplished, at least in considerable measure, sooner than anticipated. Considering the attitudes of the Department of Agriculture and the pressures for protectionism in various American quarters, which have continued to run strongly, we have come out very well indeed.

However, there was one very important aspect which, as I look back now, we did not understand very well at the time of Bretton Woods. That was the position of the under-developed countries. It is true that Keynes' buffer stock scheme was intended to help them, but it did not come to anything. We have to recognize that we really have two systems in the free world today, not one. At Bretton Woods we were looking for and we thought we were building a universal system. We have a system for the highly industrialized nations of the West which is working very well in many ways. While there are difficulties and weaknesses in the system, it has in fact made possible a fantastic growth in trade and production in the industrialized West. But this is in very strong contrast with the rest of the world. The under-developed world really is not part of this system at all. It is still far from clear how this system can be made into the universal system of trade and exchange for the benefit of the whole world. This is one of the great unfinished tasks ahead of us.

PART **2** WHAT HAS BEEN DONE?

Edward M. Bernstein

THE EVOLUTION OF THE INTERNATIONAL MONETARY FUND

There are several ways in which one can judge what the Fund has accomplished. The first is to see how the world economy has fared under the Bretton Woods system. There has been an unprecedented growth of international trade and investment; and the world has been very prosperous, at least in the large industrial countries. Without directly attributing this to the Fund, we can imply that it could not have occurred without Bretton Woods — which may be true to a limited extent.

The second criterion is to see whether the Fund has realized the ideals of Bretton Woods — orderly exchange arrangements, convertible currencies, and all that. The founding fathers had diverse views on how the Fund should work and what it should accomplish. In any case, they would not have claimed that they possessed the ultimate truth. The Fund is a quite different institution from that designed in 1944. It may on that account be better able to deal with the monetary problems of the present world than if it had been chained to the ideas of twenty-five years ago.

And that brings me to a third way of judging what the Fund has accomplished: how well has it adapted itself to the new problems that inevitably arise in a dynamic world, and to what extent has it provided leadership in devising constructive solutions to those problems? It is, of course, governments and not international institutions that are confronted with the hard, everyday problems in the monetary sphere. The Fund can advise governments on policies and it can use its resources to help them follow better policies. But its responsibility must go far beyond that. It must foresee the problems, it must understand them, and it must guide the international monetary system in meeting them.

I do not mean by this to downgrade the operations of the Fund. It has extended reserve credit in the gross amount of nearly $17.5 billion; it has approved (as of 1969) about seventy changes in the par values of currencies; it has seen thirty-four countries establish convertibility. All this shows that the Fund has performed the operations entrusted to it, not necessarily that it has been a positive force in the evolution of the international monetary system. An institution like the Fund must be judged by the ideas it generates. I propose, therefore, to examine the work of the Fund through its ideas on monetary problems and policies, and on the leadership it has provided for international monetary co-operation.

The key problem of the international monetary system is to maintain an appropriate pattern of exchange rates, particularly among the large industrial countries. There is no clear-cut statement in the Fund agreement on what is an appropriate pattern of exchange rates. For any one country it is an exchange rate than enables it to maintain a balanced payments position over an average of good years and bad, without depending on trade restrictions disruptive of international prosperity or an inadequate level of domestic demand destructive of national prosperity. However, if a country can maintain a balanced payments position only by restricting trade or by depressing employment, the exchange rate is not appropriate. In fact, the suitability of the parity of any one currency depends on the parities of all other currencies. That is to say, it is the pattern of exchange rates that must be appropriate.

The Fund agreement provides a framework of principles within which an appropriate pattern of exchange rates may be achieved. In the first place, initial parities are to be fixed by agreement with the Fund, and changes in parity are to be made only after consultation and generally with the approval of the Fund. Countries are required to maintain exchange rates within 1 per cent of the agreed parities. Finally, restrictions on current payments, multiple exchange rates, and similar departures from the rules are permissible only in accordance with the provisions of the Fund agreement or with the approval of the Fund. Frankly, these are rigorous exchange standards under any conditions. And some critics say that they are impossible standards in a world in which countries are more concerned with maintaining high levels of production and employment than with prompt adjustment of their balance of payments. It must be admitted that achieving an appropriate pattern of exchange rates is indeed very difficult in practice.

Consider, for example, the situation in 1946 when the Fund had to agree on initial parities with all its members. The European countries were then only beginning their postwar reconstruction. They were desperately short of real resources which could come only from an import surplus. What rational basis could there be for any particular parity at such a time? In fact, the Fund found a pragmatic solution to this problem. Ordinarily, the exchange rate has a dual function – it should encourage adequate exports and discourage excessive imports. In the immediate postwar period, the exchange rate could not be an effective restraint on imports – that had to be done through import controls. But even under these conditions, the exchange rate should enable a country to continue to export that part of its output that it could reasonably be expected to sell abroad. On this basis, the Fund approved the initial par values with two critical observations. First, eight or ten countries were noted where the exchange rate might soon become a barrier to the recovery of exports. Second, for many currencies it was noted that a realignment of parities would be needed when the cyclical position of the United States changed to recession.

The importance of the pattern of exchange rates in deciding on an appropriate parity was brought forcefully to the attention of the Fund in connection with the devaluations in 1949. In confidential discussions with selected European countries, all agreed that changes in parities were necessary, but the extent of the change for each currency would depend on the new parity for sterling. In the environment of 1949, when European recovery had been only partially achieved, it was impossible to make fine distinctions between the appropriate change in the parity of the Netherlands guilder, for example, and the parity of sterling. That is why the European devaluations in 1949 were nearly the same (slightly over 30 per cent) with one exception – Belgium devalued by 12.4 per cent.

There is no basis for the view that the Fund agreement imposes a straitjacket on exchange rate policy. The principle of fixed parities was adopted at Bretton Woods because that was the preference of the participating countries. The 1 per cent margin above and below parity was adopted because it was the prevailing range of exchange rates, although some US technicians favoured a broader margin. The Fund has never applied its exchange standards in a narrow way. A number of members have never fixed a parity and some have fluctuating rates, crawling pegs, or wide margins, at least between buying and selling rates. In 1949 the Fund was willing to permit Belgium to have a fluctuating rate to test a new parity. In 1950 it permitted Canada to have a fluctuating rate because of the difficulty of maintaining a fixed parity at a time of massive capital flow. The Fund staff has prepared numerous memoranda on fluctuating exchange rates; and the primary concern was not the legal position of the Fund, but the interest of its members. On this, I quote a paragraph from an early memorandum (January 1951):

If exchange rates are left absolutely free, without any intervention of the monetary authorities, there can be no manipulation for special advantages. The influence of the Fund in securing international cooperation on exchange rates would be exercised through its advice on monetary and fiscal policy. On the other hand, if monetary authorities enter the market to influence supply or demand, the degree to which they vary reserves will affect the exchange rate. By what means could the Fund under these conditions protect the genuine international interest in avoiding the use of exchange rates for purely national purposes?

The truth is that the Fund has always been permissive on exchange rate policy, except for the one principle that orderly cross-rates should be maintained. The strong support within the Fund for fixed parities with a narrow range of fluctuation reflects a conviction that such a system, with exchange rates appropriately related to the international position of countries, is conducive to economic and monetary stability. The Fund has never believed that balance-of-payments problems could be solved merely by permitting exchange rates to fluctuate. A large and persistent payments deficit is the external sign of an unbalanced economy, generally one suffering from inflation. Under such conditions, fluctuating exchange rates, particularly with free capital movements, would intensify the internal inflation, unless the monetary authorities took measures to restore stability. And if a country is prepared to follow domestic policies conducive to monetary stability, it will be able to adjust its balance of payments with a fixed parity, although not of course at an overvalued rate.

There is the practical difficulty that countries are reluctant to change the parity. For a country with a persistent dificit, this involves an admission that its policies have been wrong. For a country with a persistent surplus, this involves removing the implicit bounty that an undervalued currency gives to exporters. The Fund may in various ways exercise moral suasion on a persistent deficit country to induce it to depreciate. It has no practical means of inducing a persistent surplus country to appreciate. The recent exchange crises underline the basic truth that the parity of any one currency can be considered only as part of an appropriate pattern of exchange rates.

The experience of the past few years shows that a system of fixed parities depends upon the willingness and ability of the large industrial countries to maintain monetary stability. It is an illusion that balance-of-payments difficulties and consequent pressures on exchange rates can be avoided by in-step inflation. If the United States were to set the example of avoiding inflation, other countries might be impelled to conform to its standard. That is the only way that the Bretton Woods system of fixed parities can be expected to survive.

One of the purposes of the Fund is to shorten the duration and lessen the degree of disequilibrium in the international balances of payments of members — that is, to facilitate balance-of-payments adjustment. It is well to recall that the Fund began operations at a time when international payments were seriously unbalanced. Indeed, there was a strong body of outside opinion that the Fund should begin its operations by declaring the dollar scarce. In the view of the Fund staff, the dollar scarcity in the postwar period reflected a scarcity of real resources for European reconstruction. It manifested itself in a need for dollars because the United States was the principal source of supplementary resources. The staff held that the dollar scarcity would disappear when the European countries had completed their reconstruction and were able to compete in world markets on their customary scale — which did happen with the aid of the Marshall Plan.

The Fund needed a philosophy on the causes of balance-of-payments difficulties and on the remedies that should be applied. What troubled the Fund most about the postwar payments outlook was the danger of a protracted period of inflation. One of my first discussions with the Executive Board in 1946 was devoted to the inflation problem and the need for stringent fiscal and credit policies. In 1947, in a study of latent inflation, the staff pointed out that the financing of war expenditure by the creation of credit had caused an enormous increase in the money supply. The study concluded that the excess cash balances would not be absorbed by the growth of the economy, but would be activated gradually in higher prices and wages. In 1952, in a paper on inflation and development, the staff said that whatever the immediate cause of excessive spending, it could not be financed without the creation of money and that 'in the end, the monetary authorities are the ones that bear the responsibility for a continuous inflation. They alone have the power to limit credit expansion.'

Some months before the widespread devaluations of September 1949, the Fund considered the first proposal for a change in par value. There was nothing remarkable in the observation that the devaluation was necessitated by the cumulative effects of a prolonged inflation. The novel aspect in the analysis was the conclusion that devaluation would not restore the balance of payments unless it was accompanied by policies to reduce domestic demand to a level consistent with an appropriate payments position. The devaluation itself could have only a minor effect in holding down the growth of expenditure relative to output. The real remedy would have to be fiscal and credit policies to restrain demand. The function of the devaluation was to permit the balance of payments to absorb the output released by such measures.

Until a few years ago, it could be said that the adjustment process was working reasonably well. Where an effort had been made to restore the balance of payments either through a change in parity or through domestic policies, it had been successful. France in 1958-9, Italy in 1963-4, and Germany in 1965-6 had all achieved a prompt turnabout from a payments deficit to a surplus. The United States had a remarkable increase in its trade balance between 1960 and 1964, although this was offset by the enormous rise in US foreign investment. The failure of the adjustment process is a recent development. It is seen in the large and persistent deficit of the United States, in the inability of the United Kingdom to restore its balance of payments despite the 1967 devaluation, in the recent payments difficulties of France, in the very enormous surplus of Germany and Japan on goods and services, and in the recurrent exchange crises.

The controversy regarding recent balance-of-payments difficulties has been marked by futile discussions of the respective responsibility of surplus and deficit countries. The adjustment process is not a matter of equitable sharing of responsibility, but a practical problem of restoring a balanced pattern of international payments with a minimum of disturbance to the world economy and to the international monetary system. Of course, if the deficit country is inflating or the surplus country is deflating, the first steps must be to halt the inflation and deflation. If the distortion in the pattern of international payments is due to an inflated level of prices and costs, there will have to be a change in parity in the deficit countries. A surplus country does not ordinarily have an obligation to appreciate its currency unless there has been a structural change in its real international economic position. Finally, if the deficit country is the United States and the adjustment of the balance of payments requires a depreciation of the dollar, it is inevitable that it will have to be accompanied by a complete revision of the pattern of exchange rates among the large industrial countries.

Under the classical gold standard, the gold reserves of a deficit country were reduced and those of a surplus country were increased. As the money supply was closely linked to gold reserves, there was a monetary expansion in the surplus country and a monetary contraction in the deficit country leading to consequential changes in the balance of payments. This was the adjustment mechanism under the classical gold standard. The responsibility for restoring the pattern of international payments was not shared in an equitable way between the surplus country and the deficit country. Instead, the burden was shared in proportion to the size of the country. A country like the United States bore much less of the burden of adjustment than a small country. Of course, if a large country permitted a persistent inflation, it would ultimately have to deflate in order to protect its gold reserves and to maintain the gold value of its currency. The Bretton Woods system modified this mechanism by excluding deflation as an acceptable means of restoring the balance of payments. What are the principles of adjustment implicit in the Bretton Woods system and how do they apply to deficit countries like the United States, the United Kingdom, and France, and to surplus countries like Germany and Japan?

First, the surpluses of Germany and Japan are the counterpart of the deficits in other countries, and the problem of adjustment is to restore a balanced pattern of international payments. The surplus or deficit of each country is primarily caused by its own policies and its own economic situation, but it is also affected by the policies and economic conditions in other countries. The United States must, of course, stop generating inflation; but it cannot undertake deflation. There has been a structural change in the international economic position of Germany and Japan. Apart from their lesser inflation which has improved their price-competitive position, the world demand for their exports is growing more rapidly than their demand for imports. The D-mark and the yen will have to be appreciated to an appropriate relationship to the dollar and other currencies.* The balance of payments of the United States may have deteriorated so much that it may be impossible to eliminate the deficit without a devaluation of the dollar. If this happens, other countries will have to adjust the parities of their currencies to an appropriate relationship to a devalued dollar and the revalued mark and yen.

There is an urgent need to develop better concepts on the adjustment

---

* Editors' note: The mark was allowed to fluctuate from 30 September to 26 October 1969 after which a new parity was established at 3.66 marks to the US dollar, an appreciation of 9.3 per cent. After another period of a floating mark from May to December 1971, a new central exchange rate was fixed at 3.2225 marks to the US dollar, an appreciation of 13.6 per cent. The central exchange rate for the yen was also appreciated by 16.9 per cent relative to the US dollar in December 1971.

process. This cannot be done in the OECD. It will have to be done in the Fund. The principles of adjustment implicit in the Bretton Woods system, as I have stated them, may not be entirely correct and they can certainly be refined. It may not be amiss to point out that the practical problem of securing international co-operation in restoring a balanced pattern of international payments would be very much simpler if the United States and other deficit countries would not delay unduly in taking remedial measures before the inflation becomes built into the structure of their economies.

An international monetary system based on fixed parities must have adequate resources to meet temporary deficits until the balance of payments is restored. All of the proposals before Bretton Woods contemplated that the new institution would provide supplementary reserve facilities. The discussions were about the amount of resources and the nature of the facilities. On the magnitude of the resources, opinion ranged from a relatively small amount (originally about $5 billion) proposed by the United States to a very large amount (approximately $28 billion) proposed by the United Kingdom. Canada favoured a moderate amount of resources ($8 billion) with provision for augmenting them. For political as well as economic reasons the United States had to have a limited commitment to underwrite postwar deficits. In the end, the resources initially provided to the Fund were about what was proposed by Canada.

The other problem was whether the resources of the Fund should be available to members as a form of reserves or reserve credit. The United Kingdom wanted them to be almost the equivalent of reserves. The United States wanted them to be used for reserve credit. In fact, there is no sharp line between reserves and reserve credit. Although a country's own reserves are at its free disposal, in practice it cannot run down its reserves to an indefinite extent or for an indefinite time. Reserves must be restored if a fixed-parity system is to function effectively. However, reserve credit may be available almost automatically and with repayment geared to the restoration of the balance of payments, which may be a long or a short period. Or reserve credit may be available only under rigorous conditions with prompt repayment in a short period. The United States favoured strict supervision on the use of Fund resources, but easy terms on the period of repayment.[1]

---

1 In testifying before a congressional committee, Mr. White spoke of a repayment period of seven, eight, or nine years. This was completely in opposition to the views of his principal technical advisors who regarded a much shorter repayment period as essential.

The question whether countries have a right to use the Fund's resources within quota limits has been frequently debated by the executive directors. The differences on this issue in the early years of the Fund arose from a hard view by the United States that drawings by European members were not justified — in 1948 because their currencies were overvalued, and after 1948 because the Marshall Plan made such drawings undesirable. This was not the opinion of the staff. A second difficulty arose from a proposal by the United States in 1951 that members drawing on the Fund should undertake to make repayment within a period of three to five years. The justification for this approach was that the automatic repurchase provisions were not applicable to the United Kingdom. The staff did not object to requiring repayment within three to five years, but it did not think this should be done through a formal undertaking equivalent to a loan agreement. It proposed instead that the schedule of charges (interest on net borrowing) be raised so that the critical interest rate (4 per cent) at which a member must agree with the Fund on repayment would be reached in three and one-half years or less, instead of seven years. The Executive Board approved both the three- to five-year repayment commitment and the new schedule of charges.

Drawings on the Fund came to a virtual halt from 1949 to 1955. If countries were to have a reasonable idea on what help they could expect, it was essential to clarify the policies on the use of Fund resources. In 1952 the staff proposed that drawings equal to a country's net creditor position (the gold tranche) should be given the overwhelming benefit of the doubt. This was practical assurance that a country could regard its net Fund position as the equivalent of reserves. In the course of the next few years, the policy was developed that, as a country drew successive credit tranches from the Fund, it would have to meet increasingly stringent tests that it was using the Fund's resources to restore its balance of payments. With the development of these principles, and the termination of the stop on European drawings after the end of the Marshall Plan, the Fund resumed its operations on a normal scale. The Suez crisis of 1956-7 provided the occasion for implementing the new policies on drawings, with the Fund supplying the United Kingdom, France, and Egypt with the resources to meet their post-Suez problems. In recent years, the operations of the Fund have been on a very large scale, with the United Kingdom a particularly heavy borrower.

There have been several innovations in the use of Fund resources. In 1949 Mexico requested that it be given a contingent right to draw one-fourth of its quota in the first credit tranche, and the Fund agreed that it would not object if Mexico established a new parity for the peso and followed appropriate fiscal and credit policies. This was not quite a standby agreement, but it did recognize the importance of giving a member assurance. The present system of standbys, proposed but rejected before Bretton Woods, began with an arrangement with Belgium in June 1952. As developed, a standby gives a member the right to draw on the Fund for an agreed amount over an agreed period, subject only to maintaining formal eligiblity under the Fund agreement. Standbys have become a common method of providing assured access to the use of Fund resources in excess of the gold tranche.

Another innovation was a policy permitting more favourable access to Fund resources by countries suffering a shortfall in export receipts, mainly as a consequence of a decline in raw materials' prices. Countries depending on exports of primary products do have much larger changes in their exports than the industrial countries.. As these less-developed countries generally have relatively small quotas and are not well supplied with reserves, a change in world markets for primary products can have a serious effect on their capacity to import. The problem was stressed by the UN Commission on International Commodity Trade and by the Organization of American States. In 1963 the Fund made special arrangements for providing reserve credit to offset a decline in export receipts with somewhat greater assurance of drawings for such purposes than to meet other payments difficulties. The terms for compensatory export credits were further liberalized in 1966. The Fund also agreed to enlarge the quotas of countries exporting primary products to give them greater access to the use of its resources.

The legal problem on the use of Fund resources was finally settled in 1967 by the Amendment to the Fund Agreement authorizing the establishment of the Special Drawing Account for SDRs. Drawings within the gold tranche are now recognized as a legal right, so that members can include their net creditor position with the Fund as part of their reserves. Apart from the gold tranche, a member has no absolute right to draw on the Fund without its approval, and the Fund cannot change its present rules on drawings within the successive credit tranches. In practice, members are well informed whether a request for a drawing will be approved by the Fund. With the establishment of the Special Drawing Account, it is logical for the Fund to make a clear distinction between SDRs, which are reserves, and drawings on the general account which are reserve credit. The Fund has reached the right place on the use of its resources, but only over a long and hard route.

The discussions on the right of members to use Fund resources caused considerable, and for the most part, unnecessary controversy in the Fund. It would have been far better if the question had been approached with less emphasis on legal rights and more on practical economic grounds. The staff certainly favoured more liberal use of Fund resources in its early years. In any case, the rules that were evolved are reasonable and give members the necessary assurance on their access to Fund resources. The Fund also showed great technical ingenuity in devising methods for making greater use of currencies other than the US dollar and in facilitating repurchases by other countries, when the dollar was no longer eligible for this purpose, through technical drawings by the United States.

The provision of new reserve facilities was an essential feature of all proposals that preceded Bretton Woods. Most countries regarded the Bretton Woods quotas as on the low side. There was provision, however, for a quinquennial review of quotas. The first such review was made in 1949-50 and the staff recommended doubling the quotas to take account of the change in circumstances since Bretton Woods. The Managing Director and the Executive Board decided that this was inopportune. The second review of quotas was made in 1954-5 by the Executive Board, but was abandoned when the United States and the United Kingdom announced that they would not accept an increase in their quotas. In the 1959 review, however, the Fund recommended a 50 per cent general increase in quotas with special increases for small countries and Canada, Germany, and Japan. In the 1964 review, the Fund recommended a 25 per cent general increase in quotas, again with special increases for some countries. The general and special increases in quotas and the quotas assigned to new members raised the resources of the Fund from less than $8 billion in 1947 to over $21 billion prior to the quinquennial review of 1969.

The question of the adequacy of members' reserves, as distinguished from Fund resources, came before the Fund very early. Inevitably, the dollar scarcity was regarded by some people as evidence of the inadequacy of reserves. The Fund staff did not accept this view; but it did hold that reserves were not plentiful and that they were highly concentrated in the United States. In 1952, at the request of ECOSOC, the Executive Board instructed the staff to make a new review of the adequacy of reserves. The staff report came to the conclusion that in each of the major regions, except the United States and Canada, and in a majority of the countries in each region, reserves were inadequate to maintain a system of multilateral payments without recourse to restrictions imposed for balance-of-payments purposes. It did not take up the question whether the future growth of reserves would enable members to restore their reserves to an adequate level. Regrettably, the Executive Board approved a bowdlerized version of the staff report which was transmitted to ECOSOC and published in *Staff Papers*.

The next occasion for the study of international liquidity occurred in 1956 and was undertaken at the request of South Africa. The report, entitled *International Reserves and Liquidity*, was issued in September 1958 as a staff document on the responsibility of the Managing Director, whose views it really represented. According to the report, the adequacy of reserves depends on many factors, particularly on the willingness of countries to follow sound policies. 'If the need for flexible fiscal and credit policies countinues to be accepted in many countries, if overambitious investment plans beyond the power of available financing are avoided, and if the international institutions are able to fulfil the role assigned to them, there is nothing in the overall reserve position to indicate that present reserves are inadequate.' As for the future, the report said 'the reserve problem that the world will face in the next decade does not, therefore, appear to be insoluble ... [The] problem is not so much one of finding the resources in gold and foreign exchange which would be available for an improvement in the reserve position, but rather of the willingness of countries to take the necessary steps in the fiscal and credit fields to restore a proper balance within and among their various economies.' The one positive conclusion was that the Fund's resources were probably not adequate for meeting the reserve credit needs of its members.

In a seminar at Harvard in October 1958, I gave my views on the reserve problem:

The more important question is not whether reserves are adequate now [1958], but whether the growth of reserves is likely to match the needs of an expanding world economy ... The payments position of many countries is now sufficiently strong to enable them to accumulate reserves ... The question is whether they can succeeed in acquiring the reserves they need without weakening the position of other countries whose reserves are not excessive ... The increase in reserves that can come from newly-mined gold and a payments surplus with the Communist bloc is probably quite limited during the next few years. Any substantial improvement in the reserve position of other countries can come only from a reduction in US gold holdings and an increase in foreign official dollar balances ... [This] is not the best way of meeting the long-run problem of reserves. The time has come to place the growth of world reserves on a more rational basis, related to the new institutional developments [the IMF] and to future needs.

What troubled me most in 1958 was the danger that with the United States in deficit, the Fund would not have sufficient usable resources of surplus countries to meet the needs of its members in a time of crisis. An increase of quotas, while desirable, would not improve the liquidity of the Fund, as it would increase the quotas of potential deficit countries by much more than the increase in the Fund's holdings of the currencies of potential surplus countries. The solution I proposed was to have the large industrial countries undertake to provide the Fund with supplementary resources through loan commitments; and in a report for the Joint Economic Committee of the US Congress (January 1960), I recommended that the commitments be $6 billion. In September 1961 the Fund gave its support to this proposal and in 1962 the Group of Ten agreed with the Fund on the General Arrangements to Borrow, with the aggregate commitments of $6 billion. The Fund had recourse to such borrowings in 1964 and on two occasions thereafter.

The Fund lost the initiative on the reserve problem because of its 1958 report. The new ideas for the orderly growth of reserves came from outsiders — some of them former members of the Fund staff. Robert Triffin, with his proposal for converting the Fund into a central bank empowered to create reserves through loans and investments, was particularly successful in capturing the interest of the academic community and the press. My own proposal for a reserve unit, underwritten by the Group of Ten and issued in specified amounts at regular intervals to meet the trend need for a growth of reserves, was directed to central banks and ministries of finance. At this time, the focal point for the study of reserve problems was not the Fund but the Group of Ten. In 1965, however, the Fund again asserted its primary responsibility in this field. M. Schweitzer proclaimed that reserves are the business of the Fund, that all countries should participate in the creation of new reserves, and that this should be done through the Fund or a Fund affiliate.

There is always a considerable lag between ideas and action, and the lag is inevitably longer when it involves such a far-reaching change as the creation of reserves. Fortunately, the secretary of the US Treasury, Henry H. Fowler, recognized the urgency of the problem and proposed the preparation of a plan for reserve creation that could be activated promptly when needed. While there was general agreement on the need for a new reserve facility, there were differences of opinion on the nature of the new reserve asset, on the conditions that should govern its issue and use, and on the scope of participation. These differences were reconciled and agreement was reached in 1967 on a new reserve facility in the form of Special Drawing Rights, open to all members of the Fund and administered by it through a Special Drawing Account. The Fund took a leading part in formulating the plan for SDRs and in assuring the participation of all its members.

The Amendment to the Fund Agreement establishing the new reserve facility is the most important development in the international monetary system since Bretton Woods. The power to create fiduciary reserves is an awesome responsibility. In discharging this reponsibility, the Fund can learn from its own experience. The SDRs should be activated as promptly as possible. In determining the amount to be issued, the Fund should take a long-run rather than a short-run view. It is more important to establish confidence in the new fiduciary reserve than to have a large and sudden increase in reserves merely for the dramatic announcement effect. The issue of SDRs in the first five-year period should be sufficient to provide for the growth of aggregate reserves at a moderate rate. This would mean an issue of about $2.5 billion a year in the first five-year period.* There will be time enough for greater boldness after countries have learned to use SDRs in conjunction with gold, dollars, and other reserve assets.

A fair evaluation must conclude that on the whole the Fund has been well informed on the monetary problems of the postwar period, that the staff has been very competent in its technical analyses, and that it has often been ingenious in devising means for dealing with these problems. It is necessary, however, to make a distincition between the staff of the Fund, including its officials, and the Executive Board. The responsibility of the staff is entirely to the broad international interests of its members. Inevitably, the Executive Board is concerned with the national interests of the members they represent. The Fund itself is founded on the premise that the common interest of all countries in a workable international monetary system far transcends conflicting national interests. This is, indeed, generally true. Nevertheless, there are occasions when countries press their national interests in the Executive Board, sometimes with an exaggerated notion of how important the issue really is.

I do not mean to imply that the Executive Board, despite the responsibility of each of its members to a particular country or countries, has been parochial in its outlook. Far from that, the need to function as a board does

* Editors' note: The initial allotment made in January 1970 was $3.4 billion and $3 billion each for 1971 and 1972.

impress on members the importance of agreeing on policies in which national interests tend to be subordinated to international interests. But it is very easy to confuse what seems important to a country at a particular time with an eternal principle. The European members of the Executive Board, for example, favoured a liberal policy on drawings in the early years of the Fund, while the United States favoured a very conservative policy. More recently, the reverse has applied. The United States once supported the policy that newly-mined gold should not be sold in premium markets because it deprives the monetary system of reserves. Now the United States supports the policy that newly-mined gold should be sold in premium markets and not acquired by the Fund or by central banks. Making allowance for such aberrations, the Fund has functioned remarkably well as an international institution guided by international interests.

The existence of the Fund has made international monetary co-operation on complex problems a matter of everyday business for its members. The international monetary system of today is not precisely the system that was planned at Bretton Woods. It has been evolving over the past two decades and most rapidly in the past ten years. That evolution is dramatically evident in the operations of the Fund, in the increase in its resources, in the General Arrangements to Borrow, in the network of swap agreements among central banks, and above all in the creation of the new reserve facility. Admittedly, the evolution of the Bretton Woods concepts is less evident in exchange policies, in the techniques of balance-of-payments adjustment, and in the co-ordination of national credit policies.

The evolution of the international monetary system would not have been possible without the Fund. The Fund made change respectable because it built steadily on the existing international monetary system without abandoning it. Because the Fund favoured gradual evolution, it retained the confidence of its members — the bold ones that hope for rapid reform and the cautious ones that fear radical change.

It is not my task to discuss the future. I am sure that the evolution of the international monetary system is not at an end. The leadership in this evolution must come from the Fund. It must exercise its leadership by being flexible but fair in applying its standards, diligent in its search for new means of attaining its objectives, and, above all, completely devoted to the common interest in an international monetary system capable of meeting the needs of an expanding world economy.

66

DAVID W. SLATER / COMMENTARY

Dr Bernstein's paper is particularly interesting because it draws together ideas from the professional literature on international monetary affairs and the practical experience of a man who has an intimate knowledge of the post-war institutions, particularly the Fund. It is always interesting for outsiders to compare the general literature on the theory of balance of payments and foreign exchange and the views of practitioners. I was very much impressed on reading Mr Bernstein's paper with his intermixing of theory and practice. On reflection this may not be so surprising because I am sure that Mr Bernstein directly, and through some of his friends, has stimulated and inspired many of the best articles on balance of payments and foreign exchanges in the recent professional literature.

One of the great debates about balance of payments has been on the relative emphasis to be given to inflation versus structural factors as causes of balance-of-payments difficulties. Bernstein now emphasizes the inflationary causes and especially points to the role of monetary authorities in financing, by credit creation, the excessive demands placed upon economies. From this he then infers that exchange rate adjustments by themselves cannot correct balance-of-payments disequilibria. He insists on combinations of activities to control levels of expenditure and mechanisms to adjust the structure of relative prices as necessary means of adjustment. In this way he sets forth what I understand to be the central philosophical position adopted by the Fund throughout most of its history, in both analysis and policy. Bernstein's paper is particularly interesting as an example of up-to-date sophisticated balance-of-payments theory because of the integration he makes of income theory, asset and monetary theory, and the economies of choice and allocation. He seems to show that the ideas that guided the Fund's operations were consistent with the modern, widely respected academic literature on international economic adjustment, embodied, for example, in the works of Harry Johnson and Robert Mundell. The founding fathers of the Fund and observers of its performance and prospects emphasized the need for a continuous learning process in the ideas, analysis, and policies of such an institution. Bernstein's paper suggests that in the evolution of the Fund during the last quarter-century there has been a close relationship between the ideas and operations of the institution and the best of the new professional published economic literature on the subject.

While generally admiring the sophistication and consistency of Bernstein's argument, a few paradoxical features of his paper should be noted. First, he rather emphasizes the asymmetry between the position of surplus and deficit countries regarding exchange rate adjustment and other features of adjustment processes. He especially makes the point that neither self-interest nor external pressure is particularly effective in bringing surplus countries toward active programmes to contribute to balance-of-payments equilibrium, especially programmes involving adjustment in exchange rates. By contrast he suggests that deficit countries are, by self-interest and by exposure to pressure, the major contributors to adjustment processes, and thus likely to use exchange rate devaluations. This asymmetry is a well-established theme of the literature on the subject. Yet when we turn to the contemporary problems of exchange rate adjustment, the United States as the deficit country has long argued against a devaluation of the dollar and for a revaluation of the currencies of the surplus countries such as Germany and Japan. The paradox arises, therefore, that the greatest need for initiatives in adjusting exchange rates lies with the contemporary surplus countries while they are the least likely to act.*

The second paradox noted in Bernstein's paper concerns the creation of liquidity. In describing the various proposals put forth by the Fund's staff (and I take it by Bernstein himself when a member of the Fund staff) concerning the expansion of quotas, it appears that they have believed for a very long time in the insufficiency of international liquidity. Yet how do we reconcile Bernstein's concern for inflation as a cause of balance-of-payments difficulties and an expansionary attitude toward international liquidity? Would not an easing in international liquidity merely add fuel to the already strong and nearly universal inflationary pressure of the last seven or eight years? Indeed, in general, how can an insufficiency of liquidity be reconciled with observations of continuing rapid inflation?

Thirdly, Mr Bernstein seems to agree with Mr Rasminsky and Mr Deutsch that there has been a very considerable international monetary success during the postwar period and, in particular, success of the Fund, of the balance-of-payments adjustment processes, and of the series of exchange rate adjustments up to the early 1960s. But we must then face the paradox of apparent lack of success and repeated increasing crises in international monetary and balance-of-payments adjustment experience in the most recent years. Bernstein gives us only one explanation of the difference between the

* Editors' note: In December 1971, as part of the major readjustment of currencies, the US dollar was devalued in the sense that the dollar price of gold was increased from $35 an ounce to $38.

early successes and the later failure, and that is American inflation. It is true that he implicitly puts a little weight on some other explanations such as the slowness in developing new remedial measures, improvements of liquidity, and increased exchange rate flexibility. But I do not think he provides us with an altogether satisfactory explanation of the contrast he draws between relatively good international monetary experience before 1964 and poor performance since then.

Another paradox in my view is the all-or-nothing approach which Bernstein adopts at one point in the paper regarding exchange rate flexibility. He seems to suggest that the only choices open are a shiftable peg system on the one hand and flexible rates on the other. To be fair to Bernstein I think he does take an open-minded position with respect to exchange rate systems. But at one point in the paper he stresses a dichotomy of extremes, a choice of either rigidly fixed rates or complete flexibility. At that point he takes a view that interventions by the national monetary authorities within a generally flexible system will be very unsatisfactory. A somewhat rhetorical question is posed as to how the International Monetary Fund would defend international interests against narrowly focused national self-interest when individual national monetary authorities intervene within a nominally flexible exchange rate system. It seems to me that Bernstein presumes that the interventions by national monetary authorities in exchange markets will almost inevitably be chauvinistic beggar-thy-neighbour national self-seeking, with no regard for the international consequences. This appears to generalize too much from the unsatisfactory national performances of the 1930s to our contemporary situation. National interventions in exchange markets that occur nowadays seem to take place within the framework of a highly developed system of international economic co-operation. If a greater flexibility of exchange rates is developed within such a framework, then it may be both necessary and tolerable to have some patterns of national interventions in exchange markets rather than a complete flexibility.

There are a number of other puzzles about Bernstein's paper. Why did he not tackle the perennial questions about the propensity to international economic crisis that is alleged to be inherent in the existing shiftable peg system? Why does he not address himself to the instabilities that are associated in the 1960s with Euro-dollars and Euro-currency markets, especially the question of the relationships of the operations of international corporations to these instabilities?

Finally, I am a little puzzled about Bernstein's comparisons between the gold standard and the international monetary system under the Fund arrangements. He suggests that the only difference is that the Fund system is a gold standard constrained never to introduce deflation anywhere in the system. At other places in the paper he has made the point that inflation is the root cause of balance-of-payments disequilibria and distortion. If Bernstein believes that the present system is a gold standard that cannot permit deflation anywhere, yet he thinks the system is running into fundamental difficulties because of inflation, then it seems to me that he must ultimately come up with some proposal of major reconstruction of the system. I wonder if the reconstruction by means of internationalization of the creation of the reserve base will meet this fundamental conflict.

Raymond F. Mikesell

THE EMERGENCE OF
THE WORLD BANK AS A
DEVELOPMENT INSTITUTION

My terms of reference for this paper are to deal with the appropriateness of the World Bank for handling postwar problems in financing reconstruction and development and, in particular, to discuss the suitability of the Bank for meeting the problems as they were conceived at Bretton Woods and as they actually emerged. If those of us who were at Bretton Woods had been insulated from all knowledge of the World Bank since 1944 until the past year or two we would probably deny its parentage. It was narrowly conceived in terms of the reconstruction problems of World War I and of the concept of development assistance prevalent in the 1930s. Its immediate task was to provide reconstruction capital for devastated countries on liberal terms, largely by guaranteeing private international loans. But its role during the reconstruction period was a minor one since the large financial requirements for reconstruction were met by bilateral assistance under the Marshall Plan and other programmes. Furthermore, the management of the Bank concluded that the procedure of guaranteeing private international loans would be more costly and less suitable to carrying out the Bank's functions than that of making loans directly out of its paid-in capital and borrowed resources. At the insistence of Keynes, the principle of limited paid-in subscriptions and severe limitations on their use was adopted at the Bretton Woods conference. This meant, in effect, that the Bank's resources were to be obtained largely from the private capital markets rather than from member governments, a fact which helps to explain the conservative lending policies initially adopted by the Bank.

Not only were the resources of the Bank grossly inadequate for financing postwar reconstruction, but the project loan approach set forth in the Bank's charter was ill-suited for meeting the capital requirements of Western Europe. Of the more than a half-billion dollars in loans made to Western Europe during the 1947-50 period, most were general purpose or balance-of-payments loans. After the inauguration of the Marshall Plan in 1948, the Bank announced that for the time being it would not make further large loans to Western Europe and, since most of the Marshall Plan aid took the form of grants, Europe obviously preferred to obtain its reconstruction financing from the United States. It should also be said that large amounts of grant and loan funds, exceeding the entire capital of the Bank, were made available by the US government for reconstruction in the early postwar period before the Bank was ready for business.

In the field of loans to the developing countries, the Bank got off to a slow, cautious start. By the end of 1950 it had authorized $350 million in loans to the underdeveloped areas, of which only $100 million had been disbursed. By contrast, the Export-Import Bank of Washington alone had made loans totalling nearly $800 million to the countries of Latin America, Asia, and Africa between V-J Day and the end of 1950. By mid-1954 the World Bank had made less than $800 million in loans outside of Europe, Japan, Australia, and South Africa. During the fiscal year ending 30 June 1958 there was a dramatic rise in the Bank's lending activity from a level of about $400 million annually, which had been maintained for the three previous years, to over $700 million, two-thirds of which went to the underdeveloped regions including over $200 million to India and Pakistan. With the organization of the Bank's soft-loan affiliate, IDA, the Bank's loan authorizations have continued to grow, and during the fiscal years 1966-8 World Bank and IDA loan authorizations averaged about $1 billion annually, the vast bulk going to the developing countries.

Both the Bank and the Fund were born in a period of enormous and urgent world economic problems for which they were neither designed nor prepared to handle. Like generals, economists plan for the last postwar period. Moreover, these multinational institutions could have only limited relevance so long as the vast bulk of the wealth and economic power of the free world was held by one nation. To my mind the IMF became a truly international monetary institution only after the United States began to worry about its own balance of payments. History may record that the World Bank rose to a position of leadership in the field of development assistance *pari passu* with the declining role of the United States in foreign aid.

The Bank was designed to supplement the flow of private international capital to developing countries for financing specific projects, mainly infrastructure. It was the drying up of this kind of capital during the 1930s that motivated and directed the concept of the development functions of the Bank. The Bank was certainly not designed to meet the challenge of the post-war social and political revolution involving the poorer two-thirds of the world.

What the developing nations required was not simply an institution in Washington to which their officials could come hat-in-hand with a briefcase full of well-formulated engineering plans and economic feasibility studies for a power plant or a highway as a basis for negotiating a loan which met traditional standards of bankability. Rather, they required an institution which was prepared and equipped to involve itself in all aspects of the process of social and economic progress — in short, a development institution. In his statement before the United Nations Economic and Social Council in 1950, the president of the World Bank, Eugene Black, emphasized that the reason why the Bank had made so few loans to developing countries 'has not been lack of money but the lack of well-prepared and well-planned projects ready for immediate execution.'[1] Likewise the *Third Annual Report of the Bank, 1947-48* detailed a number of obstacles in the developing countries to the making of well-conceived, bankable loans, including the shortage of skills, the low level of education and of physical productivity, and the lack of well-formulated development plans and projects. While few could doubt the existence of these obstacles, what was lacking during the early history of the Bank was the concept of the Bank's function in helping to remove them.

Over the past two decades the Bank has gradually expanded its development services and broadened the concept of its role as a development institution. In 1949 it sent its first economic survey mission to Colombia headed by a Canadian-born economist, Dr Lauchlin Currie. This was the first of a series of technical missions, the purpose of which was to help countries formulate investment programmes which indicate priorities among the important sectors of the economy and to make recommendations on a variety of economic policies. Over the years the Bank has participated in sectoral studies in depth in member countries, many of which have led to the financing of a series of projects in such fields as electric power and transportation. Members of the Bank's staff have served as economic or planning advisers to several

1 Statement before the Economic and Social Council of the United Nations, Lake Success, New York, 16 February 1950

governments and from time to time the Bank has sent resident advisers to work directly in the governments of member countries. The Bank has also broadened the areas in which it makes loans from an initial heavy concentration in electric power and transportation to an increasing emphasis on agriculture and education. In order to provide certain types of financial assistance not authorized by the articles of agreement of the IBRD, the Bank played a leading role in the establishment of its two affiliates: the International Finance Corporation (IFC) which makes loans and equity investments to private industry without a government guarantee, and the International Development Association (IDA) which makes loans to governments without interest and with a maturity of fifty years. There were many more innovations by the Bank in expanding its financial and technical services to the developing countries, but I want to devote the remainder of my discussion to certain broad issues in the field of development assistance as they relate to the Bank, or more properly to the World Bank Group.

During the 1950s there arose an important debate regarding the approach to development assistance. Development theorists had formulated economic growth models which gave a primary emphasis to capital as the determinant of the rate of economic growth. In their development plans, countries established as the primary target a certain rate of growth in per capita GNP . The function of external financial assistance was to bridge a calculated gap between domestic resources available for investment and the level of investment necessary for the economy to grow at the target rate. It was recognized that internal and external capital resources must be allocated in a manner which would yield the expected increments to the national product, but this condition tended to be subordinated to the objective of providing a flow of capital to the developing countries consistent with target rates of growth. The apostles of capital-centred growth were therefore scornful of the bankable project loan orientation of the World Bank and argued for both a liberalization of the Bank's lending policies and the establishment of a United Nations development financing agency to make loans and grants on a scale which would assure the realization of minimum growth targets for all developing countries. For example, in 1949 a report by a group of experts appointed by the Secretary General of the United Nations recommended that the World Bank make loans for 'general development purposes not only in special circumstances but generally.'[2] In commenting on this recom-

2 *National and International Measures for Full Employment*, Lake Success, NY
1949, p. 92

mendation before the UN Economic and Social Council, the World Bank president, Eugene Black, stated that a loan for general purposes 'really means a loan for a purpose or purposes unknown.'

During the 1950s there were a number of proposals for international and regional development financing institutions which would provide financial assistance on terms and conditions far more liberal than those imposed by the World Bank. One of the best known of these proposals was that for the establishment of a Special United Nations Fund for Economic Development (SUNFED) which was made in 1953 by another experts group appointed by the Secretary General of the United Nations.[3] The desirability of such an institution was debated for years in the United Nations, but the United States and certain other developed countries took a firm position against it, partly on the grounds that an institution which would be controlled largely by the developing countries themselves would be unable to maintain high performance standards in the distribution of financial assistance, and partly on the grounds that there was no shortage of external capital in relation to the capacity of developing countries to make effective use of it. Moreover, the World Bank continued to argue that the principal limitation on the flow of development financing was not the supply of funds but the effective demand as determined by the capacity of the developing countries to absorb capital.

By 1957, however, the World Bank began to express concern in its annual reports and elsewhere over the capacity of some of the Bank's members to service additional indebtedness. This concern grew over the years and was a major factor in the Bank's taking the initiative in the organization of the International Development Association (IDA) which was inaugurated as a soft-loan affiliate of the Bank in September 1960. Like the Bank, however, IDA was established as a project-lending institution and the main difference in the lending criteria of the two institutions lies in the fact that IDA loans can be made in situations where the ability to service debts appears less promising.

I want now to examine the situation of the World Bank in the context of the history of development assistance since the mid-1950s. At the beginning of the Eisenhower administration in 1953, a decision was made to terminate the US foreign economic assistance programme and to leave the business of development assistance to private foreign investment and to the World Bank. Even the Export-Import Bank which had been lending at an annual rate ex-

3 *Report on a Special United Nations Fund for Economic Development*, New York 1953

ceeding that of the World Bank during the early 1950s was directed to limit its loans to those which were in the special economic or political interest of the United States and that 'except in special cases, should not make loans within the purview of the IBRD.'[4] However, the politics of the Cold War, plus a growning sense of international economic responsibility within the Eisenhower administration, thwarted efforts to withdraw from bilateral economic aid. The realization by the Secretary of State, John Foster Dulles, of the implications of the reduced role of the Export-Import Bank for US-Latin American relations resulted in a lifting of the restrictions on Export-Import Bank loans to the developing countries in 1954 so that in the fiscal year ended 30 June 1955 the Eximbank authorized nearly $650 million in credits, largely to developing countries. Moreover, instead of liquidating bilateral aid under the Mutual Security Administration (MSA), aid to the developing countries was substantially expanded from the level reached during the Truman administration, and in 1957 a new US government soft-loan agency, the Development Loan Fund (DLF), was established. Thus in the fiscal year ended 30 June 1959 loans by the DLF and the MSA to developing countries outside of Western Europe totalled some $530 million. US bilateral economic assistance to the developing countries in 1959 exceeded by a substantial margin the credits extended by the World Bank, and much of this bilateral assistance took the form of soft loans. Meanwhile the flow of official bilateral aid to the developing countries by other industrialized countries had reached nearly $2 billion per annum and total net official bilateral grants and loans from the OECD countries exceeded $4 billion in 1959 as against World Bank disbursements that year of $583 million.

While during the 1960s the loans and other development assistance activities of the World Bank group continued to increase, its relative share of the total aid flow was diminished by the expansion of US aid under the Kennedy and Johnson administrations, by the rise in bilateral aid from the other industrialized countries, and by the loans from the Inter-American Development Bank which began operations in 1960. In most years during the 1960s disbursements of the World Bank group to the developing countries have averaged less than 10 per cent of total bilateral and other multilateral assistance to the developing countries.[5]

4 See testimony of Samuel C. Waugh, president of the Export-Import Bank, in *Hearings*, Committee on Banking and Currency, US Senate, 84th Cong., 2nd Sess., 8 June 1956, pp. 21-2. See also my *Public International Lending for Development*, pp. 53-5

5 *Development Assistance Efforts and Policies, 1968 Review*, Paris 1968

Nevertheless we cannot measure the strength and influence of development institutions by the aggregate volume of financial flows. The estimates of official bilateral aid cover a broad range of transactions including supplier credits made by government agencies, surplus agricultural commodity sales for local currencies, and economic support of countries like Vietnam and Korea engaged in war or bearing heavy defence burdens. Much of this aid makes little or no contribution to basic economic development. True development assistance is not simply the provision of resources; it is the promotion of development objectives through a variety of measures including financial aid. We must therefore look at the position of the World Bank in terms of its influence and leadership role in the world development assistance effort generally.

With the inauguration of President Kennedy in January 1961, the United States government launched a broad development assistance programme and, in effect, assumed a strong leadership position for the promotion of social and economic progress in the developing countries. In his dramatic foreign aid message of 22 March 1961 Kennedy stated, 'The 1960s can be – and must be – the crucial Decade of Development – the period when many less developed nations make the transition into self-sustained growth ... Our job in its largest sense is to create a new partnership between the northern and southern halves of the world, to which all free nations can contribute, in which each free nation must assume a responsibility proportional to its means.' Special attention was given to Latin America and at the Punta del Este Conference in August 1961 Kennedy pledged to assist the Latin American countries in the achievement of a number of specific economic and social goals, including a minimum rate of growth in per capita output of 2.5 per cent per annum. To this end the administration agreed to underwrite a flow of capital to the Latin American countries 'from all external sources during the coming ten years of at least $20 billion ... ' and 'the greater part of this should be in public funds.'[6]

There are three points to be noted about America's foreign aid posture in the early 1960s which have a bearing on the role of the World Bank. First, there was a complete reversal of the 1953 policy which had attributed the major responsibility for public development assistance to the World Bank. In fact, there was a gradual retreat from this position throughout the Eisenhower administration but much of the rationale for us bilateral aid was

6 The Charter of Punta del Este, August 1961. *Alliance for Progress*, Washington, DC 1961, pp. 9-24

couched in terms of US national security. Second, the United States not only expected to provide the largest share of the financial assistance for development, but it had established sizable aid missions in a large number of countries in Asia, Africa, and Latin America which maintained continuous contact with, and influence on, the development policies of the foreign governments. Thus the United States established itself as the chief co-ordinator of development assistance both at the country level and in the co-ordinating committees of representatives of US and multilateral aid institutions in Washington, DC. In stating this I do not overlook the fact that the World Bank sponsored and chaired consortia of donor countries and had a limited number of country representatives of its own. But with the notable exception of certain African countries which maintained close economic and political ties with the European powers from which they had recently become independent, the US economic missions constituted the predominant external influence in the developing world. Finally, AID adopted a philosophy of development assistance which differed significantly from the basic approach of the IBRD and this philosophy was reflected in AID's operations.

Let me expand a bit on this last point. Although AID's activities encompassed a hodgepodge of foreign assistance, including surplus agricultural commodities (PL 480), supporting assistance for countries subject to external and internal communist aggression, project loans, balance-of-payments assistance, emergency aid, programme loans, and technical and financial aid for education, health, and housing, the underlying rationale of AID was the principle of self-sustaining growth. The Program Coordination Staff of AID, initially under the direction of Hollis B. Chenery, sought to programme assistance in accordance with a growth model which projected a path leading to self-generating growth – a condition whereby the developing country would in time generate sufficient savings and foreign exchange income to maintain a target rate of growth in output per capita without further external aid.[7] Country performance in accordance with the model depended upon the behaviour of the savings and investment ratios and other parameters. Given certain social and institutional constraints, progress toward the self-generating growth goal depended upon the country's taking certain self-help measures, such as the avoidance of inflation and the proper allocation of capital on the one hand, and a critical level of capital inflow over a requisite

7 A full exposition of the model which in considerable measure guided the policies of AID's Program Coordination Staff may be found in H.B. Chenery and A.M. Strout, 'Foreign Assistance and Economic Development,' *American Economic Review*, Sept. 1966, pp. 679-733.

period on the other. Now this view of the aid process not only satisfied the orderly constructs of the economic model builders, but it was in accord with the traditional American view that foreign aid should have a predictable termination date. International charity to help people to help themselves had broad public acceptance but a dole of indefinite duration was unthinkable.

The orientation of the World Bank has been quite different from that of AID. In the first place the Bank is a permanent institution. Relatively poor countries will always be with us and the World Bank is under no compulsion to work itself out of a job. The Bank provides its capital both to poor countries just emerging from a primitive state and to countries like Mexico and Taiwan whose future progress and prosperity seem assured. True enough it has a soft-loan window to provide concessionary loans to countries with limited capacity to service external debts, but there is no termination date in IDA's charter either.

The World Bank's operations have not been guided by any particular growth or development model. In its country evaluation reports the Bank examines the general policies and economic prospects of the country and seeks to identify the appropriate development strategies and the policies for implementing them as a guide to its lending policies and recommendations. In those cases where the Bank, either on its own or as the manager of a consortium or consultative group, has become the major factor in the supply of development finance, it tends to become deeply involved in advising with regard to the country's development planning. In general, however, the Bank has eschewed any identification with target rates of growth or the achievement of a condition of self-generating growth. Basically the Bank is prepared to lend its capital to countries that can make effective use of it and where such capital cannot be readily obtained on reasonable terms in the private capital markets.

Since the mid-1960s there have been three developments which have altered significantly the relative role of the World Bank in development assistance. First, both the relative and the absolute financial contributions of AID have been declining since fiscal year 1966 when that agency's net obligations and loan authorizations reached a high of $2.5 billion plus Food for Peace assistance of $1.5 billion. By fiscal 1968, AID's loan authorizations and obligations had declined to $1.9 billion and AID's budget was subjected to substantial cuts in 1968. Moreover, in view of the apparent policy of the Nixon administration favouring private foreign investment and multilateral aid over US bilateral assistance, it seems likely that AID's relative role is destined to continue to diminish.

Second, there has been a steady increase in the lending activities of multilateral agencies during the 1960s not only by the World Bank Group but by the Inter-American Development Bank (IDB) inaugurated in 1960 and more recently by the Asian Development Bank. In 1968 the IDB was lending at the rate of nearly a half-billion dollars annually and this rate is expected to increase in 1969. Like the World Bank Group, the IDB makes both hard loans and loans on concessionary terms.

Third, the World Bank Group itself, in addition to nearly doubling its lending activity since 1959, has been exhibiting a growing concern and sense of responsibility for the development problems of the poorer countries of the world. I think there has been a gradual broadening of the horizon of the World Bank over the past five years which has revealed itself in several directions. For one thing, the Bank's annual reports and major addresses by World Bank officials have been stressing the need to increase the flow of resources from the industrialized countries to the developing countries and in particular the need for untied loans available at low or no interest charge. In place of the complaints about poor planning, poor project preparation, and low debt servicing capacity as limiting the loan operations of the Bank — which characterized the Bank's official utterances during the early 1950s — there has been increasing emphasis on what the Bank and other institutions should be doing about obstacles to development and to the flow of development assistance. In 1961 the Bank established a Development Services Department to administer the technical assistance work of the Bank and its liaison activities with other organizations such as the UN Development Program and the UN Food and Agricultural Organization. The early 1960s also saw the Bank heavily engaged in the organization of consortia and consultative groups for co-ordinating and mobilizing external assistance to individual countries.

Shortly after he became president of the Bank, George D. Woods substantially expanded the research activities of the Bank concerned broadly with economic and social development as contrasted with project evaluation. In 1964 he established the position of the economic adviser to the president with Irving Friedman as the first incumbent and reorganized and expanded the research work of the Bank in a new Economic Department headed by Andrew Kamarck. The Economic Department has assembled an impressive group of internationally recognized economists and other social scientists who work on problems of economic and social development. The Bank's economic staff has had a major influence on the evolution of the Bank as a development institution and on development policies generally through their writings and contacts with other development lending agencies. In 1965 the

Bank published the preliminary results of a study by the Bank's economic staff designed to determine how much additional capital the less developed countries might productively use between 1965 and 1970.[8] This study concluded that the less-developed countries might use an additional $3-4 billion annually beyond what they were currently receiving. In commenting on this conclusion the Bank's president stated that it was his deep conviction 'that the present level of finance is wholly inadequate, whether measured by the growth rate which the advanced countries say they are willing to facilitate or in terms of the amount of external capital which the developing countries have demonstrated they can use effectively.'[9]

The publication of this finding is of special interest since in the past the Bank's staff had tended to be critical of the estimates made by the United Nations' agencies of the flow of external capital required to achieve minimum growth targets. The UN estimates were usually based on aggregative growth models from which were calculated the gaps between required levels of investment and domestic savings or required levels of imports and foreign exchange earnings for the achievement of target growth rates.[10] The approach employed by the Bank's staff in arriving at its own figure of additional external capital for the developing countries has been characterized as the 'capital absorptive capacity'[11] approach and may be contrasted with the gap model approach employed in the UN estimates. The Bank's estimates were determined by individual country studies in depth, taking into account the public investment programmes and estimating the cost of the projects and programmes which in the judgment of the Bank's country specialists met certain standards of technical and economic feasibility. Similar estimates were made for major industries in the private sector. The capital absorptive capacity approach is of course in line with the Bank's traditional project orientation, but the significant departure from the past in putting forth these estimates was the admission on the part of the Bank that the major limitation on the flow of development financing was in the *supply* of external resources

8 See World Bank and IDA, *Annual Report 1964-65*, Washington, DC 1965, p. 62
9 *Statement of George D. Woods, President, World Bank Group, to the Ministerial Meeting, Development Assistance Committee, Organization for Economic Cooperation and Development*, Paris, 22 July 1965, p. 5
10 See, for example, United Nations, *Studies in Long-Term Economic Projections for the World Economy*, New York 1964, pp. 67-8
11 See John H. Adler, *Absorptive Capacity: The Capacity and Its Determinants*, Washington, DC 1965

rather than the capacity of the developing countries to use them productively.[12]

The Bank's concern with the debt service capacity of developing countries has been reflected in its vigorous efforts to expand the contributions of the developed countries to IDA, and the transfer of some of its earned surplus on World Bank loans to IDA, and by its emphasis in recommendations to developing countries on the importance of broadening their export base. At the request of the UNCTAD Conference in 1964, the World Bank staff undertook a study of the problem of fluctuating export receipts of developing countries. In their report to UNCTAD the Bank's staff formulated an imaginative proposal for assisting countries experiencing unexpected shortfalls in export receipts where such shortfalls limited the ability to fulfil development programmes.[13] The Bank promoted acceptance of this proposal at the UNCTAD II meeting in New Delhi in 1968 and in informal discussions with government officials. In the same field, the World Bank in association with the International Monetary Fund is engaged in the preparation of a study of price stabilization for primary products for submission at the annual Board of Governors meeting in the fall of 1969.

The inauguration of Robert McNamara as president of the World Bank in April 1968 has given promise of a new era in the history of the institution. The growing debt service problems of the developing countries, the failure of the development decade to achieve its goals, the lagging interest in foreign aid on the part of the governments of the developed countries, the disappointing results of UNCTAD, and the erosion of the leadership role of the United States left a sense of despair and a leadership vacuum in the whole postwar movement to promote economic and social progress in the developing countries. In an obvious effort to project the Bank into a position of leadership, Mr McNamara made the following statement at the annual meeting of the Board of Governors last September:[14] 'What can the Bank do in this situation? I have been determined on one thing: that the Bank can and will act; it will not share in the general paralysis which is afflicting aid efforts in so many parts of

---

12 For a discussion of the World Bank's method of calculating the $3-4 billion of additional external capital as contrasted with the gap model approach, see E.K. Hawkins, 'Measuring Capital Requirements,' *Finance and Development Quarterly* (a journal published jointly by the International Monetary Fund and the World Bank Group), no 2, 1968, pp. 2-7
13 See *Supplementary Financial Measures*, Washington, DC 1965
14 *Address to the Board of Governors by Robert S. McNamara, President, World Bank Group*, Washington, DC; IBRD, 30 Sept. 1968, p. 4

the world. I do not believe that the Bank can go it alone and do the job of development that needs to be done around the world by itself; but I do believe that it can provide leadership in that effort, and can show that it is not resources which are lacking – for the richer countries amongst them have resources in plenty – but what is lacking, is the will to employ those resources on the development of the poorer nations.'

Mr McNamara outlined an action programme by the Bank for the medium-term and appointed former Canadian prime minister, Lester Pearson, to head a commission of world leaders to survey the development needs for the remainder of the century and how they can best be met.[15] On the basis of a survey of development potential and capital absorptive capacity over the next five years, the Bank Group in 1968 established a goal of lending twice as much over the next five years as over the previous five-year period. As stated by Mr McNamara, 'this means that between now and 1973 the Bank Group would lend in total nearly as much as it has lent since it began operations 22 years ago.'[16] As a further indication of the Bank Group's broad approach to development, McNamara stated that the Bank would give special emphasis to education, agriculture, and population control in its technical and financial assistance.

Of course this ambitious programme for the Bank will depend upon its ability to market its securities and on the willingness of developed countries like the United States not only to subscribe their allotment to the current IDA replenishment but perhaps to a still larger third replenishment of IDA's resources.[17]

I want now to turn briefly to some of the development assistance problems that call for the exercise of leadership by the World Bank Group if it is to fulfil the role envisaged by its president. The number of multinational and national foreign assistance agencies has increased substantially in recent years so that the sources of aid which may be available to an individual recipient have become exceedingly diffuse. There are several regional development banks, some of which, like the Inter-American Development Bank and the Asian Development Bank, raise their own funds from the sale of securities

15 The idea of this Commission was first suggested by Mr Woods. See *Development – The Need for New Directions*, an address by George D. Woods to the Swedish Bankers Association, Stockholm, 27 October 1967 (published by the IBRD)
16 Address to the Board of Governors, 30 Sept. 1968
17 The second general IDA replenishment as approved by the Board of Governors calls for annual contributions of $400 million for three years beginning November 1968. The total US contribution is established at $480 million.

and contributions from governments, while others, such as the Central American Bank for Economic Integration, depend upon external institutions or governments for their loan funds. In addition, there are a number of agencies providing technical assistance such as the UN Development Programme and the UN Food and Agricultural Organization. Finally, there are several aid coordinating organizations such as the Inter-American Committee on the Alliance for Progress (CIAP) and the Development Assistance Committee (DAC) of the OECD. There is an important role for DAC in exhorting the developed countries to meet the goal of contributing 1 per cent of their national incomes to the flow of resources to the developing countries and in seeking to improve the quality of aid. There is also a special role for regional co-ordinating agencies such as CIAP.[18] However, the most urgent and important problem in the area of aid co-ordination lies in the mobilization and concerted management of the various aid sources at the country level.

One of the most important functions of a development assistance institution is to influence the policies and development strategies of aid recipient countries. This requires among other things a periodic analysis and evaluation of the country's economic and social progress as a basis for recommendations by the development institution; the promotion of self-help measures and improved economic performance on the part of the aid-recipient; and the systematic use of lending policy to influence the allocation of the country's available resources for the carrying out of development strategies. This important developmental function cannot be adequately performed where several agencies with differing lending policies and country evaluations are operating independently of one another in the same country. The World Bank Group, AID, and other assistance agencies have sought to deal in part with the problem of aid co-ordination by means of consortia of donors such as exist for India and Pakistan, or by the organization of less formal consultative groups as in the case of Colombia and Nigeria. But the consortia have not achieved co-ordinated aid management which involves, or should involve, continuous contact with, and surveillance over, the aid programme, and above all the power to withhold or alter aid flows as an instrument for influencing policies. The consortia are often little more than a

18 CIAP was established to co-ordinate development assistance to the members of the Alliance for Progress and to prepare reports on the development progress of Latin American countries to be used as a guide by the principal agencies providing financial aid including the IDB, AID, and the World Bank Group.

group of donors that pledge a certain amount of aid after a general review of a country's programme and the list of external requirements presented by the government. Such arrangements can scarcely be satisfactory to donors that are interested in performing a development assistance function along the lines I have just outlined.[19]

There are several obstacles to the establishment of centralized management of aid from several donors at the country level. For bilateral donors at least, aid is an instrument of foreign policy and, in addition, much that goes by the name of aid constitutes credits for the promotion of the exports of the donor. Regional agencies such as IDB do not operate in a political vacuum and often find it difficult to insist upon reasonable performance standards on the part of the larger and more powerful borrowing countries that exercise considerable influence in the agency. AID has been able to perform a co-ordination role with reasonable effectiveness in countries where it has been the predominant donor and where it has had an adequate staff operating in the country. In the Latin American area the Bank has worked with the other development assistance agencies, the IDB and AID, through CIAP as the co-ordinating agency. The CIAP model has much to recommend it since CIAP is an organ of the Latin American countries themselves and the United States. However, CIAP needs to be strengthened substantially before it can serve effectively in co-ordinating lending policies of aid agencies at the country level. I do not know whether it is politically feasible for the World Bank to assume the role of aid co-ordinator in many or any developing countries, but I do believe that an effective world leadership role in the field of development assistance would require it.

One final note. The Bank's leadership role will, I believe, require that the World Bank Group become more fully internationalized. Originally the only national subscriptions which the Bank was able to use without restrictions were those of Canada and the United States, and the World Bank was virtually limited to borrowing in the New York capital market. Now the Bank's capital comes from all over the world. Its image as a rich nation's club dominated by the United States certainly needs to be changed[20] in the interest of increasing the influence of its development policies and recommendations.

19 For a critical review of the operations of consortia and consultative groups see John White, *Pledged to Development, A Study of International Consortia and the Strategy of Aid*, London 1967
20 This point was made by a former official of the World Bank, Escott Reid, in his book, *The Future of the World Bank*, Washington, DC; IBRD, September 1965, pp. 19-23.

GRANT L. REUBER / COMMENTARY

I should point out at the beginning that for me the Bank and the Fund originated in a lecture hall rather than in the conference rooms from which the Bretton Woods Agreements emerged. Nor can I claim to have had any direct experience with these institutions.

Let me also say immediately that I found both papers highly informative and perceptive. Not only have the authors provided a useful summery of the evolution of Bank-Fund operations during the past twenty-five years, but also they have provided a valuable personal assessment of these operations. It is particularly noteworthy that, writing independently, both authors focus on one central criterion for judging Bank-Fund activities – namely, the intellectual leadership provided to the international community by each institution in its respective field of interest. I entirely agree that this is the primary criterion to be used for evaluating the Bank-Fund performance in the past. It is also, I believe, an appropriate point of departure as we consider how these institutions might be improved in future years. This is not to suggest that the many other aspects of the operations of these institutions are unimportant. However, if one is concerned with the evolution of these institutions, I believe the central issue concerns their thrust as intellectual forces in those areas with which they are primarily concerned.

How successful have the Bank and the Fund been when judged on this basis? This question obviously does not lend itself to a straightforward yes or no answer. Both authors suggest that their performance might have been better. Mr Bernstein illustrates this by the way in which the Fund missed the bus on the international liquidity problem: it was surpassed by people outside official circles as well as by official groups operating outside the Fund in such forums as the Group of Ten. In the case of the Bank, I think the failure to provide greater leadership is perhaps best illustrated by its preoccupation with the bankability of projects and its failure to think and act as a *bona fide* development agency.

This leads to an important question that has not been as directly faced in these papers as I hoped. Why in the past have the Bank and the Fund not provided greater intellectual leadership in their respective fields and what might be done to improve the performance of each institution in this respect? Both authors make a number of suggestions that bear indirectly on this, but I do not think either of them faces it head on. There are many possible explanations. For example, it may reflect the constitutional arrangements that apply to each institution. Or it may reflect the outlook and approach of those who manage the institutions. Alternatively, the operating and administrative responsibilities of these institutions may constrain the development of ideas within each institution, by comparison to the ideas explored by freer spirits outside the institutions. Then, again, the performance of the Bank and the Fund may reflect what some might regard as the predominance of a central bank — treasury view of the objectives of economic policy and how the instruments of policy can best be deployed in the pursuit of the objectives of policy. Whatever the answer, I think these and similar questions need to be explored when we are concerned about the improvement of these institutions, particularly as sources of intellectual leadership in those areas with which they are concerned.

The remainder of my comments relate to the Bank and are addressed particularly to Professor Mikesell's paper. As Mr Deutsch rightly pointed out, satisfactory international financial machinery still remains to be constructed as far as the less-developed countries are concerned and this task falls primarily, though not entirely, within the purview of the Bank.

Professor Mikesell notes there has been a steady trend in the direction of making the Bank a more effective development agency; and this development appears to have been enhanced by the appointment of Mr McNamara as president of the Bank. As the Bank takes on an increasing role as a development institution, there are several aspects of its activities that presumably will be expanded. One of these relates to the level of aid flows; another concerns ways and means of improving the planning and administration of aid allocations; and the third relates to increasing the flow of private investment to developing countries. These are obviously very large questions that I can only inject at this point and cannot discuss. There are, however, a few points that I would like to raise specifically in relation to the planning and administration of aid where I believe the Bank may have a particularly important role to play as far as moderate-size donors such as Canada are concerned.

As foreign aid programmes have grown in size and in complexity it has become more important and more difficult to ensure that these programmes are well run — well run in the sense of allocating the aid in some rational way reflecting notions of using the funds well and making aid available on satisfactory terms. By functioning as a development agency I think the Bank can play an important role in co-ordinating the aid efforts of individual donors and particularly of moderate- and small-size donors. In addition, the Bank can help to infuse a much greater input of information, research, and ideas into the planning and administration of aid in these donor contries than it has in the past. One would hope that a more closely co-ordinated approach would avoid such curious anomalies as, for example, the situation where moderate and small-sized donors sometimes have had more money available to spend on aid than they had reasonable projects on which to spend it. One way, for instance, by which the Bank might expand its re-sources would be to farm out projects to individual donors rather than under-take them itself. In addition, the Bank might assist donors by directly helping with the appraisal of programmes and projects. (There is, of course, all kinds of informal communication between the Bank and individual donors, but I am talking about something more substantial than that.) In addition, by exploiting its relationship with donors more effectively, the Bank might be able to assist in liberalizing the terms on which aid is provided. At the cost of some exaggeration one may say that in the past the Bank seems to have oper-ated too much like any other donor and has not assumed the larger catalytic role that might appropriately have been expected of it.

There are many other questions that might be raised as well. There is, for example, the question of investment in infrastructure as compared to invest-ment for other purposes. The present mechanism of providing aid has grown up under a system where the main emphasis has been on investment in infra-structure. It may well be that in many countries, after twenty years of aid receipts, the emphasis might usefully be modified to give greater priority to investment in 'productive' purposes. This may call for quite a different vari-ety of aid outlets. This is an area in which the Bank has already made im-portant contributions and these presumably could be extended.

Professor Mikesell raises another range of issues in his paper concerning the question of whether it is more satisfactory to follow what one might call a 'project approach' as compared to the broad 'development strategy ap-proach' that has become associated with the names of Chenery and Strout.

Finally, I fully agree with what Professor Mikesell says about one of the important functions of the Bank in trying to rationalize and co-ordinate much of the activity that goes into investigating projects and investigating countries. One can certainly sympathize with a developing country that is continually faced with a series of visiting teams investigating various aspects of its economy. Much of the time and energy that goes into this activity may have a very low rate of return. Presumably the Bank could, as Professor Mikesell points out, serve a very important function by rationalizing some of this activity and co-ordinating it more closely.

In summary, the main point I want to raise as far as the Bank is concerned is how effectively and how rapidly the Bank could transform itself from what it now is — and it is, I fully accept, a very competently staffed and well-run institution — into a full-fledged international development agency.

PART **3** SPECULATIONS AND FUTURES

Robert A. Mundell

THE FUTURE
OF THE INTERNATIONAL
FINANCIAL SYSTEM

The Bretton Woods twins were conceived during a world war that followed a world depression. They were created by men who hoped to make the world depression-proof. We have not had a great depression since the war but have suffered the opposite malaise of inflation. Nevertheless, the twenty-five years since the founding have been years of prosperity unparalleled in history. It would be hard to say how much credit is due the Fund and Bank for this prosperity, but that fact alone should make us cautious about unbridled criticism. We do not know what would have happened had the Bretton Woods Agreement not been ratified, but the fact that the Fund has presided over a remarkable era in economic history shifts the burden of evidence onto the Fund's critics. I include myself in the latter group, but primarily because we want to see the present era of prosperity continue and I believe reform of the Fund can enhance the chances that it will.

I shall not, unfortunately, speak of the World Bank or the problems of the less-developed countries. The sad fact is that these countries have not shared sufficiently in the prosperity of the past twenty-five years. I do not believe the developed countries have contributed enough of their resources, either financial or intellectual, to these countries. But those problems will be raised by Dr Prebisch. I want to concentrate on the past, present, and future of the international monetary system.

There are two approaches to a study of the future. We can turn to history and look for repetitions and recurrent events. We can also use theory (which, however, is ultimately based on recurrences in history) to try to discover the laws of evolution of the data to be explained. This is not easy in the case of the international financial system because the number of complete cycles in the system has been small. We have not experienced sufficient repetition to gain high confidence probabilities in evolutionary theories. Our understanding of the future must, therefore, rest in the realm of enlightened conjecture.

It will be useful to make a distinction at the outset between a monetary *system* and a monetary *order*. A system is an aggregation of diverse entities united by regular interaction according to some form of control. When we speak of the international monetary system we are concerned with the mechanisms governing the interaction between trading nations, and in particular between the money and credit instruments of national communities in foreign exchange, capital, and commodity markets. The control is exerted through policies at the national level interacting with one another in that loose form of supervision that we call co-operation.

An *order*, as distinct from a system, represents the framework and setting in which the system operates. It is a framework of laws, conventions, regulations, and mores that establish the setting of the system and the understanding of the environment by the participants in it. A monetary order is to a monetary system somewhat like a constitution is to a political or electoral system. We can think of the monetary system as the *modus operandi* of the monetary order.

We are accustomed to thinking in terms of a given monetary system. In what follows I shall have to treat as variables what are usually, in economic analysis, regarded as constants. But the system may be undergoing change without our noticing it. The 'monetary order' may be rigid and unable to cope with the problems of the new system. If we fail to distinguish between *system* problems and *order* problems we may wrongly discard ideas about the system that no longer appear to work, or blame the order because it was created to house a system that had grown beyond it. In the latter case we have to ask whether it would be better to strengthen the order and suppress changes in the system, or modify the order to accomodate changes in the system.

I shall organize my subject first by glancing at the past from the standpoint of the historical procession of systems and orders, and then consider some aspects of future prospects and needs of the world economy and of our intellectual attitudes.

Let us consider the subject in its historical perspective. It is not possible to specify a date at which the 'international financial system' began. Its origins, like that of trade itself, are shrouded in obscurity. Received doctrine is a compromise between inaccurate literary works and numismatic finds. The Phoenicians probably had a fairly smoothly working system around the time of the discovery of Europe. And after them the Etrurians, the Egyptians, the Lydians, the Greeks, and the Romans. The Chinese and Japanese also had established monetary systems before the Christian era, but the time they started to engage in international trade is debatable.

Starting with the gold coinage of Julius Caesar, however, a very explicit monetary order was established throughout the Roman empire. There is a continuity in this order that lasted twelve centuries, a continuity ensured by a union of the altar, the throne, and the purse. None of the Christian princes of Europe dared to strike gold coins; they all implicitly recognized the suzerainty of Constantinople, although Charlemagne did set up a satellite monetary system based on silver. Only after 1203, with the sacking of Constantinople by the Crusaders, did the western princes truly become kings and strike gold coins. This occurred long after the military and political authority of Byzantium had declined and was instigated by the religious competition of the western pope and the economic competition of Venice.

The monetary *system* used in Europe, however, was a mixed system between the time of say Justinian the Great in the sixth century and the sacking of Constantinople. Gold was the *international* money of this Roman period; the princes struck silver coins, and the lesser vassals copper and tin coins for home use. The coinage hierarchy corresponded somewhat to the feudal hierarchy. Toward the end of the seventh century, however, the *domain* of the Roman order declined, as a competitive monetary order arose out of Islam when the caliphate challenged the authority of the Basileus by striking a gold dinar competitive with the bezant. The threat to the Christian monetary order was considered such a sacrilege that it led to the outbreak of new wars in the 690s between Christendom and Islam. But the Moslems held firm and the universality of the Byzantine order was broken. The Byzantine gold bloc was encircled by the Moslem silver bloc for most of the period which the historians of Northern Europe somewhat parochially refer to as the Dark Ages; scattered remains of dinars have been found in that great arc stretching from the Pyrenees to Scotland through Scandinavia and the Baltic-Samarkand trading routes to North Africa. These two monetary orders coexisted for about five centuries.

We can look at history as a sequence of changes in the monetary order or changes in the domain over which it has authority. I have already mentioned the change when the Byzantine monetary domain was challenged by the Moslems and the occidental system was split. Changes that were, in a sense, more important occurred as the new emerging nations of Western Europe began to strike their own coins. The Byzantine order itself broke down completely in 1203 and led to the fluctuating exchange rates of the Middle Ages.

The collapse of the order, however, did not mean that world trade could do without an international money. Dominant moneys arose to become what Carlo Cipolla calls the 'dollars of the Middle Ages.' The most important money in the thirteenth and fourteenth centuries was the Venetian ducato, but Florence and Genoa, which had developed great banking houses, became close competitors. When Spain, under the Hapsburgs, dominated Europe in the sixteenth century, Spanish money became important, being used for about three centuries; in the 1790s it became the basis for the us dollar. Dutch money had meanwhile assumed international importance after the world-wide increase in the price of gold in the 1540s, and the revolt of the Netherlands from Spain. The money markets of Antwerp and then Amsterdam dominated the European financial scene as Dutch money and banking based on free coinage secured the confidence of international investors. It was around this time that Thomas Gresham, as financial agent for Mary and then Elizabeth in the Netherlands, got the English seriously interested in international finance.

In the seventeenth century English-Dutch and Portuguese-Dutch rivalry on the high seas and in Asia and North America led to a series of wars that ended with England imitating Dutch banking techniques and importing a branch of the Dutch royal family. Prince William of Orange needed a bank to fight some new wars. The Bank of England, patterned after the Bank of St George of Genoa (founded 1407), was developed as an arm of the British government and, by the end of the wars of the Spanish succession, had established that confidence in the pound and British credit that lowered interest rates and enabled Britain to 'borrow her way into an empire.' In 1717 gold was made legal tender along with silver, and in 1774 silver was demonetized. In 1793 London's main competitor, the Bank of Amsterdam, had to close its doors, opening the way, during the Napoleonic period, for the hegemony in international finance of the City of London and a century of sterling diplomacy.

From 1820 to 1931 London was the main capital centre of the world and the pound the dominant currency. 1931 may be taken as the turning point when Britain left the gold standard. But the handwriting was on the wall two and perhaps three decades before that. Britain had achieved eminence as the major maritime power in the seventeenth and eighteenth centuries, the dominant industrial power from 1750 to 1870, and the presiding financial power from 1820 to 1914. But British domination began to weaken after 1895, with the emergence of powerful rivals in Germany and the United States and continuing competition from France and Russia who went onto the gold standard by the 1890s. The signal for the change was the peak in the price of consols. Cracks had already appeared with the strains on the British financial system after the Boer War and naval rearmament and as early as 1908 Keynes had begun his attack on established morality by advocating wider gold margins. Financial eminence, however, is based on memory, and it lives on long after political and military strength have declined, as the Byzantine, Moslem, and Spanish moneys had indicated centuries earlier.

It is this procession of dominant currencies, reflecting the actuality and the memory of the military and economic strength of the great powers, that signals for us the potential turning points of the world monetary and political system. Currencies have traditionally achieved pre-eminence by starting off strong, leading from the confidence based on undervaluation. Thus gold, a cheap means of payment for high-value contracts (as compared to silver and copper), was over-priced by Julius Caesar (the Roman ratio of gold in terms of silver was 1.2 to 1, the Indian ratio 6½ to 1) and the solidus correspondingly undervalued. The gold content of the solidus was less than its market value except at the official mint, and Gresham's Law came into operation. Usage establishes familiarity and familiarity breeds habit. Finally (provided its supply is controlled), the metallic content of a coin becomes less important than its value as money as it becomes used as a unit of account. This happended with the guilder, which was initially under-valued in the sixteenth century, then achieved prominence and could then ride along for decades on the strength of its reputation. Devaluations have to be infrequent (perhaps not more often than once a generation); and they should always be excessive. An 'overkill' is necessary to reverse expectations of weakness and restore pre-eminence.

The pound followed a course similar to the guilder, but inept British monetary policy in the twentieth century speeded the decline of the pound. A good devaluation in the 1920s (instead of appreciation) might have reinstated the pound as a strong world currency. In 1931 sterling prices could still extend over half the world. But when devaluation was tried in 1949 it did not restore equilibrium; sterling prices had become much less important than dollar prices. After 1967 the domain of sterling as a unit of account and contract began to be whittled away because expectations were not reversed, until today its domain is threatened in Britain itself.

The dollar began its role as a world currency in the 1920s, but it achieved prominence as a reserve asset after 1934 when gold was overvalued at $35 an ounce. Initially the dollar borrowed prestige from gold. But as with the pound and the guilder before it, the dollar itself assumed a role distinct from the relation it had with respect to gold. With or without gold the dollar has taken on a vitality of its own internationally, a fact not well understood by many economists several years ago who, quite rightly, had recognized the importance of gold convertibility but not the steady transformation away from the need for it. The dollar era could, by some standards, be said to have begun as early as 1945 or even 1934, but it is probably safest to conceive of its beginning in 1960, when the price of gold rose to $40 an ounce on the London gold market, but exchange rates remained unchanged. This demonstrated that during a period when gold was strong, other countries would choose to move with the dollar rather than with gold. The March 1968 communiqué* only confirmed what had become obvious long before.

Part of my task is to predict how long the dollar era will last. On the basis of historical experience one would be tempted to say one or two centuries. Of course the Roman-Byzantine order lasted twelve centuries, although its domain dwindled after the spread of Islam. The Moslem money dominated its domain for at least five centuries. The Venetian ducato was important for three or perhaps four centuries, and the Florentine and Genoese currencies for somewhat less. In more recent times the age of empires and currencies has been shorter. The Dutch era lasted effectively less than two centuries, from, say 1570 to 1750, the pax Brittanica for perhaps two centuries.

The shortening of the time span of the domination of specific currencies in recent times is probably due to the acceleration of the pace of change and the diffusion of information. The age of the dollar will be shorter than other currencies, so that it would be rash to predict a dollar age of more than one century, and perhaps wise to feel unsafe about any prediction longer than fifty years. Fortunately, it is not necessary to make such long-run predictions since the passage of time will bring us more information. If one counts 1960 as the beginning of the dollar age a fifty year period takes us to AD 2010.

* Editors' note: In March 1968, the 'gold pool' countries met in Washington and issued a communiqué which separated the official and private markets and imposed sanctions on any country that arbitraged between the two.

It may be a mistake, however, to regard the US as just another dominant country. When one takes a close look at the particular aspects of the US economy that create the conditions for American hegemony, one becomes inclined to the belief that we are witnessing something very different from just the rise of a new power to sit at the head of the table, a phenomenon quite different in kind from the countries preceding it in the leadership races of the past.

After the final breakup of the Eastern empire in the thirteenth century, one can move in a geographical semicircle, through the great powers ascending and descending the temporal landscape: Venice, Genoa, Portugal, Spain, the Netherlands, France, England, Germany, America and Russia. The current bi-polar or tri-polar world is different from the power configuration prevailing during the European civil wars. The present East-West confrontation may be more like the conflict between Islam and Christendom, leading to a cultural coexistence of two civilizations unique in kind from any preceding experience. Of course, the tremendous power to inflict mutual damage upon one another is so great that uncertainties about any prediction necessarily have to be raised. Because the phenomenon of America represents a new level of civilization one might predict that America's time span would be much longer than that of just another power. And yet, because of the revolution in destructive technology, the variance is higher.

This much, however, can be said. If we have political instability we shall surely have monetary instability. And if the United States retains its position as the dominant power the dollar will surely maintain its position as the dominant currency. The major long-run problem confronting world monetary authorities is that of building a monetary order capable of housing a system that is dominated by the growing absolute and relative financial power of the US economy in international commercial and monetary relations.

It is at this point that we turn to consider the function of a 'monetary order.' Perhaps we should ask first of all whether it has a purpose. There is no answer to this philosophical question. But it is useful, nevertheless, to suppose it as having a purpose. Its purpose is to protect the member states from the abuses of unrestrained Darwinism.

When we look back over the past twenty centuries and ask how the monetary order has been manifested in actual institutions, we are startled to find that the Bretton Woods system is unique. For there are only two previous periods in history when it could be said that a monetary order existed. One was during the Roman-Byzantine era, from the time of Julius Caesar to the fall of Constantinople; the other was the period of the international gold standard as it operated in the nineteenth century. The other periods in history lacked a monetary order in the sense in which I have defined it. Yet these two orders were of a different nature from the order created at Bretton Woods.

The Roman order was not a voluntary agreement entered into freely by member states. It was an extension of Roman and Byzantine imperialism; it might be more correct to call it a manifestation of Christian financial imperialism insofar as gold acquired a mystique and sacred character for very practical, rather than very spiritual reasons. Its sway extended over Christendom and lasted as long as Christian authority ultimately rested in Constantinople. A similar case could be made for the satellite monetary order established by the Carolingians and the competitive order established under Islam. It was the hegemony of the dominant power that enabled the monetary order to survive and the order itself was established to serve the interests of the empires in question.

The international gold standard, in contrast was again different from the Roman system. The gold standard was a set of rules, conventions, and policies. These mores, like the rules of fair play and manners, evolved haphazardly. The gold standard was never created. It was an outcome of an historical process. No one knows when it began. One can find convenient starting points in the sixteenth, seventeenth, or eighteenth centuries. Perhaps less important than the date it began was the date it was perceived and rationalized as a coherent system by, for example, Cantillon and David Hume. But it was never codified into an international agreement. The closest thing to a formal international agreement was the Genoa Conference of 1923 in which it was agreed that countries could use as reserves each other's currencies, thus ratifying what already existed: the gold exchange standard. Earlier agreements, like the Latin Monetary Union of the 1860s, were restricted in scope. The gold standard was never formalized in international law.

The first agreement of a comprehensive and binding sort in modern times was the Bretton Woods agreement of 1944. Not since the absurdly long stability of the Byzantine system could it be said that we had an international monetary 'order' until the IMF was set up. It is here that the uniqueness of the Bretton Woods agreements lies. It gave the postwar period a monetary order more comprehensive than that established during the Roman period. But there was a fundamental difference in that the Bretton Woods order, unlike the Roman order, was not established to serve the interests of an empire.

I am aware, of course, that there are differences in opinion on this question. The charge has been made that Bretton Woods was established to serve as a 'cloak for American financial imperialism,' or for the Anglo-Saxon powers. I find the charge wholly unsustainable, but it is not possible to convince those who see subtle conspiracies in every action. The US had a dominant voice at Bretton Woods, but how could it be otherwise, given the world power structure at the time and the hostilities that were still going on? The US had four basic choices: 1) no agreement at all, 2) the key currency proposal of John Williams and others, 3) an agreement like the one that actually was made, or 4) a more far-reaching cession of national monetary sovereignty such as that proposed in the Keynes plan. Either of the first two alternatives would have exposed US power more nakedly than it actually did develop, while the fourth possibility would have seen a world bank dominated by the US. To those who regard the agreements as an extension of US power one is tempted to ask: Is there any international monetary agreement that the US could have made at the time that would absolve them from 'guilt'?

I believe it is closer to the truth to say that the Bretton Woods order provided a new framework in which both big and little countries alike could find a place and protection. But it was inevitable that the dominant country would influence, even dominate perhaps, the institution. Depending on the configuration of national sizes prevailing in a particular century, that influence will be more or less dominating. Had the IMF existed in the nineteenth century Britain would have dominated it. Had it existed in the eighteenth, seventeenth, sixteenth, or fifteenth centuries, France, Holland, Spain, or Venice respectively would have been more dominant. The IMF is currently faced with precisely the problem of how to adapt to the role that, haphazardly enough, has been assumed by the US. But only the most bizarre ignorance of history could lead to the suspicion that it could be otherwise than that the dominant economy played a leading role in the operation of the system.

The world economy stumbled into the key currency system. The result was that the order and the system came into conflict. Either the order has to accommodate the position of the dominant economy, or the dominant economy has to retrench to fit itself into the system. But it will not retrench or be disciplined if its vital interests are at stake because it always has the option of abandoning the order. There are two paths. One path leads toward Darwinism expressed in the dollar standard and the exposed power of the dominant country. The other lies in the direction of international order and an attempt to harmonize, where it is possible, the interests and rights of other members of the world community with the vital interests of the dominant economy.

What are the vital interests of the dominant economy? Simply the overriding requirement of internal balance. It would do no good to devise an international monetary order that attempted to force unwanted inflation or deflation upon the United States. If this were attempted the US would probably retreat outside the domain of the order and establish its own dollar area. Subject to this accommodation, however, the US can and probably would find it in its own interest to submit to discipline intelligently administered. Recent history has seen an acquiescence of the United States to major commitments, international treaties, and agreements that have gone beyond that of any other dominant power in history, and, indeed, seen the United States accept a double-standard role imposed or conditioned by the tyranny of the weak.

Now let us consider in which direction the Bretton Woods agreements should be allowed to evolve.

I have argued before that the Federal Reserve System acts like a world central bank, and that the US dollar has most of the attributes of a world currency. The path toward a better international order leads, in my opinion, in the direction not of stripping the dollar of these roles, but increasingly internationalizing them. More specifically, it means creating a world currency freely exchangeable into dollars, and a sharing of the responsibilities of US monetary policy in an international consultative committee operating through the IMF. I believe this to be possible as long as the needs of the world economy and the needs of the US economy are not incompatible with one another. But it is up to the smaller countries to take the initiative. The IMF is their institution.

I have gone into the questions of monetary reform in detail elsewhere and I do not propose to reiterate devices or plans for reform here except to summarize the method I would adopt for creating a world currency that could operate in a world with a dominant currency like the dollar. The principle is to internationalize the dollar and to give an international authority a voice in US monetary policy.

I would have all gold and unwanted dollars earmarked (to use Dr Bern-stein's euphemism) to the IMF and exchanged for 'intors,' which the US would maintain fixed in price to the dollar. The stock of intors could then be altered in two ways: 1) issues of SDRs and 2) changes in the official price of gold. Once the gold is earmarked to the Fund the extra profits from holding it when and if its price is changed would be spread among its members. The private market in gold is kept completely separate so that the world money supply is insulated from private hoarding demands. Once the central banks have fully recognized that it is gold value and not tonnage that is required, all monetary laws prohibiting private dealings in gold can be abolished. The system would then have a fully gold-backed international money without the resource cost of producing it and the most important step would have been taken in the direction of global monetary management. The IMF would dele-gate the dominant economy to fix its currency to intors, while other coun-tries pegged their currency to either dollars or intors at their option. In-creases in world money would then no longer provide a seigniorage gain exclusively to the United States, and yet the advantages to other countries of using the New York market as a deposit centre would be retained.

I have now discussed some aspects of changes I think will or should take place in the system in the future. I want to conclude by discussing the future of ideas about the system. For the sake of succinctness I shall state my views as propositions about the future and omit the usual qualifications about a sub-ject which is, after all, highly speculative.

1 Economists will increasingly adopt the view that the advantages of a world-wide regime of flexible exchange rates have greatly diminished. There are intellectual and practical reasons for this. The case for flexible exchange rates has never been a very sound one. It is based on the Keynesian assump-tion of money illusion and fixed money wage contracts. But money illusion is rapidly disappearing because of the acceleration of the rate of diffusion of information, the increased sophistication of the public on monetary sub-jects, and the increasing awareness on the part of workers that an increased price level lowers real wages and that devaluation raises prices. This means that devaluation will quickly result in equivalent (or almost equivalent) in-creases in stock prices and commodity prices and (except for an increasingly short lag) higher wages. The implication is that cost curves will be increas-ingly set in terms of foreign currency reducing the favourable effects of

devaluation on employment and leaving the effectiveness of exchange rate changes on the trade balance dependent on the slender reed of redistribution (including real balance) effects.

2 Exchange rate variations, whether achieved through floating rates or devaluations, will be increasingly punished by flights of capital from the fluctuating currencies. Small countries that allow their rates to float or that alter parities frequently will find residents not only wanting to hold stocks of dollars, but also to use the dollars as an internal unit of account and contract. To counter this tendency internal controls will become increasingly necessary to protect the contract domain of the local currency. But the burdensome nature of these controls and the costs of enforcement will lead most of the countries back to the fixed exchange rate system. Confidence in the currency would assume paramount importance and confidence will have to be maintained by higher foreign exchange reserve ratios. Perpetual discounts on forward exchange and higher domestic interest rates will be the symbol of weakness of a currency. The costs of protecting local currencies will be aggravated in those countries that adopted flexible exchange rates or allowed crises of confidence to arise. In 1969 one saw mark loans at less than US interest rates and sterling loans at high interest rates because of the market belief in the undervaluation of the mark and the overvaluation of sterling.

3 These factors would become increasingly relevant under any size configuration of the international economy in an age of rapid information speedup. But it is accentuated by the particular circumstances prevailing in the last half of the twentieth century when dollar-denominated contracts already account for over half, and will soon, in my belief, account for over two-thirds of all (internal and external) contracts made. The attraction of the dollar, by contrast, with any currency competitive with it is so considerable that flexible exchange rates would create the risk of a steady erosion of the domain of local currencies. This erosion is present even under the present system of fixed exchange rates within the existing exchange margins, but it becomes deadly when the parity is in doubt. The wider the exchange margin the greater the difficulty of protecting the local currency domain.

4 The current interest in widening the exchange margins among bankers and exonomists may have some influence in achieving, in the real world, greater exchange flexibility in the near future, particularly because of a wide-spread belief that a realignment of parities is necessary. The belief itself is sufficient to force exchange rate or internal adjustment. However, the movement toward wider exchange margins and greater flexibility will, in the long run, lead

to *lesser* exchange flexibility. This is because it enhances, like crises, the absorption of information, and advances the death of money illusion, rendering exchange rate changes increasingly ineffectual and increasing the gyrations of the rate and the erosion of the unit of account.

5 American economists will be slower at seeing the implications of the decline in money illusion than their foreign counterparts. This is because of the perspective from which American economists view the world, and the natural tendency to project solutions good for the US economy onto other nations. Flexible exchange rates mean something very different for a dominant currency country and for the other countries. There would be no need for monetary prohibitions in the United States under a system of flexible exchange rates because the position of the dollar as a unit of contract and account is secure for decades. There is no need for American laws to forbid contracts in francs and pesos and kyats; indeed, it would be hard to arrange a gold clause in a United States contract even if it were legal to make one. But dollar clauses will have to be forbidden in any country that adopts one of the various schemes for gliding parities, sliding margins or crawling pegs.

6 A system of floating exchange rates will be increasingly unattractive to countries outside the United States. But the United States, to the extent that it does not feel threatened now by official gold conversions, already has the benefit of independence given by a flexible exchange rate. Recognition of this fact will turn the question of flexible exchange rates by 1980 into a dead issue except in countries that persist in inflating or deflating at substantially different rates from the mainstream of the world economy. But it will become increasingly expensive to depart from the norm.

7 There will be growing recognition of the fact that two paths to international monetary reform, flexible exchange rates and an increase in the official price of gold, would lead not to the solutions anticipated by their proponents but to a dollar standard. Recognition of the growing encroachment of the dollar in all areas of international finance should revive interest in the only two viable alternatives to it: internationalization of the dollar through the creation of a world currency fixed to the dollar; and a competitive money created by the European countries and possibly Japan. (Russia, however, may emerge as a factor in international monetary relations with an externally convertible rouble in the 1970s.) There are externalities to be reaped under a dollar standard that will create resistances to it and lead in the direction of a competitive bloc, or an international sharing of the advantages accruing to the US from a dollar standard. The actual outcome will depend on whether

any monetary leadership arises in Europe or from the smaller members of the IMF.

ROBERT M. STERN / COMMENTARY

Professor Mundell has painted a broad canvas depicting the rises and declines of international monetary orders from early Christendom to the present. He has also offered some tantalizing suggestions about how the present system should be allowed to evolve in the future and some ideas about how this evolution may in fact proceed. While it strikes me that he has perhaps exaggerated somewhat the significance of monetary orders and mechanisms in shaping the course of world history, I shall not engage him on this ground. Nor shall I project a half century into the future, which is about the life he assigns to the dominance of the US dollar in the international financial system. I propose instead to confine myself to a somewhat more immediate range of considerations that may be relevant to the future of the system.

First of all, it is by no means clear that the system can evolve in the way Mundell sees it unless there are fundamental changes in the attitudes that nations have regarding their sovereignty. The importance of national (and regional) sovereignty can be illustrated by the cleavages between the US and Western Europe that have been manifested at times in the periodic meetings and decisions reached outside IMF channels in the Group of Ten and the meetings of central bankers in Basel. Important national decisions have also been made in Western Europe, sometimes in direct violation of supposedly regional obligations. There are also important cleavages between the advanced industrialized countries and the less-developed countries that have been evidenced by the unpopularity of the IMF in many of the latter countries and in the recent unwillingness of the advanced countries to link new reserve creation with development assistance. The point is, therefore, that the priorities given to national interests may stand in the way of the international co-operation that is required to achieve a truly integrated and smoothly functioning international financial system.

Second, it is not clear from Professor Mundell's remarks how the adjustment mechanism can be made to operate effectively in the future. This is particularly the case since he believes that exchange-rate variations would not work for adjustment purposes because of the disappearance of money illusion. Presumably the international co-operation on monetary policy would permit interest rates to be varied especially for balance-of-payments purposes. But would not internationally co-ordinated fiscal policy be required as well? Otherwise, how could we be certain, if exchange rates are to remain fixed, that balance-of-payments adjustment can be effected without undue pressure on the level of employment in individual countries?

Third, while Mundell has cited some historical examples of Gresham's Law, he does not address himself to the possible problems that might arise when countries have the option of holding their international monetary reserves in the form of gold, dollars, and SDRs. There are some difficult technical and political problems arising from the need to make decisions concerning the level and distribution of new reserves and the relative rates of interest of the different reserve assets. Given the commitment to create SDRs and the acceptability and familiarity that may follow from their use, there may be less of a need for a dollar standard than Mundell implies, assuming that the IMF could take over more of the reserve creation that the US is now providing.

Fourth, we have witnessed in recent years very substantial short-term capital movements during periods when existing exchange parities have come into question. While the impacts of these sudden and large movements of capital have been mitigated somewhat by currency swaps and selective controls, there is, nevertheless, a potential for serious disruption that remains so long as exchange rates are fixed and there exist substantial amounts of mobile capital. Assuming that domestic conditions do not warrant changing the exchange rate and that national reserves and international credit lines are not fully adequate, some consideration might be given to a policy whereby individual countries could resort to selective taxation of short-term capital movements, subject to IMF approval. While it may be the case that such measures could not be implemented without fairly detailed exchange controls, these measures might nevertheless be advantageous in the short run if the international financial system and domestic stability would otherwise be exposed to substantial disruption.

The final point that I wish to mention concerns the policy harmonization of the level of world interest rates and national deviations from that level. I have already mentioned that other countries may not agree on a general monetary policy in which the US has the main responsibility for establishing the level of interest rates. Moreover, while other countries can devise ways for determining national deviations from the world level, it is by no means clear that they can necessarily resolve their balance-of-payments problems in this way. This is particularly the case when account is taken of the longer-run stock adjustments of capital flows and the interest costs involved. Interest rate policy may not be viable, moreover, when a country's costs and prices are out of line internationally.

It may be unfortunate, but I believe that it is still a fact of life, that countries tend to pursue national over international objectives. So long as this is the case, the international financial system will be subjected at times to important disturbances. The fact that the timing and magnitude of these disturbances cannot always be foreseen accurately means that we need standby measures that will help to promote short-run stability. It is also not clear that the adjustment mechanism can work effectively in the absence of exchange rate adjustments. Once we are on firmer ground on these matters, perhaps we can then turn to the longer-range considerations to which Mundell has addressed himself.

Raul Prebisch

A VIEW FROM
THE DEVELOPING WORLD

I want to deal with the Bretton Woods institutions from the point of view of developing countries. I do not intend to review the past evolution of those institutions, but rather will concentrate my attention on some important possible improvements in their future functioning, especially as regards Special Drawing Rights, a new supplementary financing scheme, and the financing of international buffer stocks.

The recent reform establishing the SDRs in the IMF is of paramount importance. A short while ago, when this reform was still a matter of great controversy, a group of experts appointed by the UNCTAD secretariat upon the request of member governments dealt with this subject from the viewpoint of developing countries. The experts recommended that part of the new international monetary resources created by this reform should be transferred to developing countries through the channels of existing multinational financial agencies. At that time the UNCTAD secretariat was advised not to push this matter of a 'link' very strongly, in order not to add new difficulties to those interfering with the progress of the idea of international monetary reform. But now the situation is different. The Articles of Agreement of the Fund have been amended for establishing the Special Drawing Rights, and it seems that the opportunity has arrived for giving due consideration to that idea of linking the creation of new resources with financial transfers to developing countries.

Meanwhile, this idea has been taking strides forward. Indeed, shortly after the report of the UNCTAD experts, another group appointed by the Inter-American Committee for the Alliance for Progress strongly supported the same idea. The Perkins Report, submitted to President Johnson, also recommended its acceptance. And last but not least the Reuss Subcommittee on International Exchange and Payments of the United States Congress held hearings on this matter.

That does not mean that the idea of a link does not encounter serious objections. Let me deal briefly with two of them. The first concerns the danger of creating an excessive amount of new resources, under the pressure of the enormous needs of developing countries for developmental financing. The amount of the SDR creation should respond strictly to monetary considerations and not to financial needs of developing countries, however desirable may be the full satisfaction of these needs. Undoubtedly the IMF will determine the proper criteria to avoid any excessive creation of SDR resources, and the fact that important developed countries have a clear voting majority in the IMF should be sufficient guarantee that the new system would be properly managed in this respect.

The second objection is of another character. It is argued that the measures advocated in favour of developing countries through the link will not be a mere monetary operation but a transfer of real resources to them from developed countries. And this transfer will not respond to the decision of individual developed countries but rather to the decision of an international authority — that is to say, the IMF. Let us examine this argument.

This type of international transfer of real resources is not new. It has existed historically. Gold-producing countries have always benefited from a transfer of real resources supplied to them in the form of goods and services by other countries in exchange for the new gold produced. In the present case essentially the same thing would happen with the difference that countries exporting goods and services would not receive gold but the equivalent of gold. But instead of requiring labour to produce them, they would not cost anything.

It is true that under the gold standard the production of new gold does not respond to decisions by any international authority but rather to market forces. However, it cannot be denied that the decision to maintain a fixed price for gold by governments has a considerable impact on these forces. It would be preferable to have a clear decision of the IMF in response to the monetary needs of the world rather than to events as arbitrary as the production of new gold.

In the light of what has just been said, the ideal solution to this problem of improving the world's monetary mechanism would have been the creation of new resources by the IMF and their full transfer to developing countries through the channels of existing financial agencies. This would parallel the way in which the gold standard functioned in this respect. Countries willing to get these new resources, in order to increase their monetary reserves, would have to compete for them in the world market by exporting goods and services to capture the new SDRs. So in this fashion the accumulation of reserves would depend on the export competitiveness of countries trading within a multilateral framework. But the formula that has been adopted is different. New monetary resources are distributed to member governments of the IMF in an automatic fashion, according to pre-established proportions. Some critics have expressed their concern that countries with balance-of-payments deficits would not take sufficiently strong internal measures to correct the external disequilibrium precisely because of the new resources internationally provided for them. We cannot deny that there is a certain weight to this argument and this risk could have been avoided if, instead of the automatic distribution of new monetary resources, the original pattern of the gold standard had been followed in the international monetary reform. If this had been the case, countries with balance-of-payments deficits would be forced to take measures to correct their situation and improve the competitiveness of their exports in order to obtain part of the new international monetary resources.

However, the new system could evolve gradually to this ideal. It is true that the new resources as such cannot be transferred to developing countries except by further modifying the recent amendments to IMF Articles of Agreement, which may prove to be a serious difficulty for the time being. But a parallel agreement could be established whereby developed countries receiving new monetary resources would channel an equivalent of them, in their own currencies, for financial assistance to developing countries. That does not mean that the equivalent of the full amount of new SDRs should be transferred in this way. It would not be realistic to expect this to take place while the present monetary imbalance persists. This is clearly a matter for the future. Therefore it may be more realistic to start with a proportionate transfer of these resources — say 50 per cent at the outset — and to increase this proportion gradually when the situation improves, with a view to arriving at the full transfer in the future.

Some concern has been expressed as to the real meaning of the link to developing countries in terms of providing them with net additional resources. Indeed, it may be possible that developed countries now contributing to the external financing of developing countries might decrease the present flow of their resources, thereby neutralizing the benefit accruing to developing countries. This could happen if developed countries had not accepted at UNCTAD II in New Delhi (1968) the commitment to supply to developing countries an annual amount of net financial resources equivalent to 1 per cent of their gross national product. The mobilization of new monetary resources through the link, as just explained, could contribute in an important way to the fulfilment of this commitment in the near future.

From another angle it may be said that the transfer of these new resources to developing countries through existing channels need not necessarily follow the existing pattern of lending. What I have in mind is the possibility of improving this pattern in the light of experience, introducing into the world financial mechanism the financing of international buffer stocks and supplementary financing. Developing countries have shown a great interest in these two matters at UNCTAD discussions.

When Lord Keynes dealt with his proposal for international monetary reform before Bretton Woods, he conceived the creation of a mechanism for the financing of international buffer stocks. The reasons for this are well known: an effectively functioning international buffer-stock scheme introduces an important element of regularity into the workings of a commodity market by stabilizing world prices within some preagreed range without disturbing the long-term commodity market trend. But nothing as yet has been done internationally to help finance such buffer stock schemes. In this case, as well as in the case of GATT, the problems of developed countries have always had a high order of priority while those of developing countries were considered as residual, if not ignored. However, there is now a clear change of attitude, and both the Bank and the Fund are in the process of considering this problem in response to the Rio resolution (1967) of their respective boards of governors.

It is obvious that this particular problem cannot be solved by a mechanical transfer of resources for the financing of international buffer stocks. On the contrary, this operation should be geared to a sound commodity market stabilization programme, such as the programme prepared for cocoa in UNCTAD which eliminates the risk of losses.

It is well known that there are many commodities that cannot be subject to programmes of stabilization. Furthermore, even in the case of stabilization programmes, there is always a certain margin for fluctuation of prices and of export earnings. All this means that, in order to attenuate the external vulnerability of developing countries, there is a clear need for supplying them with new financial resources when there is a serious decrease in their external income that brings with it a corresponding contraction of internal economic activity. This is the purpose of a supplementary financing plan presented to UNCTAD by the staff of the World Bank in response to the British/Swedish resolution approved at UNCTAD I (1964). The objective of this supplementary financing scheme is to protect the economic development plan of a country from serious disruptions caused by unexpected short-falls in their export proceeds. In my view this scheme is a very sound one, notwithstanding some technical aspects that could and should be improved. However, after a long discussion preceding UNCTAD II, no substantial progress has been made, except for adherence to the idea in principle. Sharp differences as to the best way of translating it into concrete form still exist, but behind these differences one can frequently detect the reluctance of important countries to commit additional financial resources while the present difficulties of those countries persist. It may be hoped that the acceptance of the link between the Special Drawing Rights of the IMF and the transfer of resources to developing countries may make practical agreement on this matter less difficult. Technical difficulties should not prove insurmountable. The World Bank has accumulated great experience in dealing with developing countries and some latitude should be given to it, whether directly or through a subsidiary, for the flexible management of this supplementary financing scheme.

It is obvious that this scheme presupposes the existence of an economic development plan, or at least a public investment programme, in developing countries. But this should not be construed as a requirement of supplementary financing. The need for planning responds to other important considerations as well: namely, to have clear economic and social objectives on the one hand and proper means of achieving these objectives on the other, following a discipline of development. Unfortunately, in this matter there are still some contradictions interfering with the idea of planning. There is, generally, a strong reluctance by international suppliers of funds to commit resources in advance for (say) a period of four or five years or for the entire duration of the plan. I refer to a commitment in principle, subject, of course, to the fulfilment of the main policy lines of the plan and the presentation of specific objectives. This reluctance is a very serious obstacle. Countries, in addition to their own reasons for planning, should have a clear external incentive. A reasonable assurance of sufficient external financial resources is needed to complement the mobilization of their own resources.

I have, as you will see, pointed out that supplementary financing and international buffer stock schemes are essentially complementary in that they both contribute, though in different ways, to attenuating the problems experienced by developing countries in adjusting their economies to unforeseen vicissitudes in export earnings. To the extent that export earnings fall short of planned targets, to that same extent the implementation of development programmes would be jeopardized. How then to ensure the external integrity of a sound domestic development plan? It would be an act of inestimable importance and great international statesmanship if the Bretton Woods institutions could associate their prestige and resources in responding to that question. Note then the organic interrelationship that could be conceived if the SDR 'link' could help the developmental requirements of the Third World, whether through strengthening supplementary financing or buffer stock schemes, or directly in the form of financial assistance to national plans.

GERALD K. HELLEINER / COMMENTARY

Most essential in any discussion of the issues raised by Mr Prebisch is the need, first, to distinguish between short-term possibilities and longer-term objectives — where we want to be in 1980 or 1990. The questions to which Mr Prebisch has addressed himself are, I think, second-best short-term possibilities. I had hoped that he would find time to say a bit more about matters relating to direct aid transfer which remains the first-best policy and the longer-term objective in the development area.

But let us look at some of these second-best possibilities. Mr Prebisch has put the case for three: aid-linked SDRs, supplentary financing, and buffer stocks. I agree with him on the need for all three of these if there is no other way of transferring resources and if these are possible. I would rather, however, have resources transferred directly, if that is also possible, through a multilateral international institution like the World Bank. Direct multilateral aid is the long-term best objective. In the absence of alternatives, however, we must, of course, work with what we can.

As far as the SDRs are concerned, I share Dr Prebisch's disappointment that the IMF, in its haste to race to the front of the international parade again in the whole liquidity question, felt it necessary to choose a compromise solution which was, admittedly, much better than the solution which would otherwise have materialized through the independent actions of the Group of Ten but which still falls far short of the best solution as far as the Third World is concerned. His explanation of the objections which prevented acceptance of the scheme for transferring resources into the developing world at the same time in which world liquidity is being increased, however, is incomplete. It was not simply that the developed world was unwilling to transfer its resources or that it feared such a transfer would lead to inflationary pressures on a world scale, so much as three other objections to the scheme which stood in its way.

First, the scheme would have involved the surrender of national control over aid distribution; this, although probably of positive world social value, was considered to be undesirable by major 'donor' governments.

Second, too easy access to increased foreign exchange reserves might hinder the imposition of economic discipline and the introduction of suitable (longer-term) strategies and development policies. I am not sure that I believe this myself but others do, and it is not an illegitimate point. The fact that there are at least ten 'steady' borrowers from the IMF in the underdeveloped world suggests that there may well be effects of this sort. I am not sure I would not favour closing our eyes to the ten steady borrowers. Let us have twenty if there is no other way of transferring resources! (Such IMF loans, though intended to ease short-term difficulties, are in practice low-interest programme loans.) The possible weakening of discipline is a point, however, that has to be answered, not only in the context of the SDR scheme but in that of all aid schemes. The provision of more reserves for aid *may* simply postpone necessary adjustments in internal policies.

Third, there is the real possibility that the provision of resources through the SDRs would not have resulted in any increase in transfers to the Third World. I do not share Dr Prebisch's touching faith in the importance of the 1 per cent of GNP aid commitment negotiated in New Delhi in 1968. There was another 1 per cent commitment at the beginning of this 'Development Decade' and, as we all know, the percentage of national income devoted to aid during this decade actually fell. I doubt whether the existence of the 1 per cent commitment guarantees, as he suggests, that increased aid provided through SDRs allocated in one way or another to the developing world would not be offset by diminished aid elsewhere.

These common reservations about the use of SDRs for development do not alter my own view that this remains a good, if not the best, approach to transferring resources for development; it is certainly much superior to the once proposed commodity standard. It is also superior, I think, to commodity agreements. It is undoubtedly superior to the International Coffee Agreement which is an odd system of resource transfer — both inequitable and probably inefficient. The distribution of real resources through the distribution of SDRs is likely to be more equitable than that achieved through any commodity scheme. Having said all that, I think that it is too soon, or too late and too soon, to discuss the use of SDRs for development except in terms of longer-term objectives because of the short-term difficulties in producing another amendment to the IMF, because SDRs are not yet actually working, and because there remains a great deal of doubt as to whether the 85 per cent vote required for activation will materialize.* A short-term possibility, however, might be for the IMF, World Bank, and IDA to exercise leadership at the time the SDRs actually come into use. Strong moral suasion could be exerted at that time upon member countries to expand national aid programmes, either through replenishment of IDA or through increased bilateral schemes. That is the time to make the case for aid if the World Bank Group and everyone else concerned with aid is ever going to make it. Perhaps that is the most we can hope for at the present.

The other two proposals discussed by Mr Prebisch, supplementary financing and buffer stock schemes, are more clearly second-best, or even third-best approaches. (If one is already considering SDRs as second-best, one would have to put the former two one notch down.) Supplementary financing is subject to the same objections as I have outlined with respect to the use of SDRs for development. Moreover, it does seem to reward bad forecasting and to offer the possibility of improper 'game-playing' on the part of economic planners. In any case, it is not going to assist those with a downward trend in their commodity prices if it is accurately forecast. It is not necessarily going to assist those with good planning or good policies either. Let me finish, however, by saying that if we have nothing else, it is much better than nothing.

Buffer stocks present the same set of problems and invite the same sorts of objections. Stabilization, which Dr Prebisch suggests is the intention of buffer stock schemes, is not, of course, the major problem. Support is the prob-

* Editors' note: Since the time of writing, a three-year planned allocation of SDRs was approved.

lem – *increased* prices, not stabilized ones. Even if stabilization were the intention of buffer stock schemes, it would be more efficient to stabilize through the provision of increased access to credit. It is simply cheaper that way. If our national policy makers do not permit increased credit or increased resource flows in any other way, however, by all means let us have some aid 'sleight of hand' through buffer stock schemes, and let us, if necessary, describe them as 'stabilization' arrangements. Other 'disguised aid' devices, may, however, prove quicker to implement and/or more effective. Recent World Bank studies, for instance, showed that the transfer of about one-fifth of the duties at present collected on tropical beverages at entry to developed-country markets would constitute quite a large addition to the aid flow into the developing countries. (One-fifth transfer would create twice the effect on export earnings as would total elimination of these duties.) If one is prepared to work on buffer stock sorts of aid schemes, one must open the door to many other aid proposals. It may be that schemes for collection of taxes on an international level earmarked for aid, for instance, are as fruitful a line to push as buffer stocks.

I do want to make my position clear. I want these second- and third-best approaches if there is nothing else. But why can't we try to think a little bit more about the role of the World Bank Group, other aid bodies, and the possibility of increasing resource flows through more direct channels? Is it more difficult for us now to raise direct-aid contributions or to devise new tricks to provide aid-in-disguise? We are expending an awful lot of effort trying to devise all sorts of second- and third- and fourth-best schemes. They make a lot of work for economists, but they are *so* inefficient. How much easier it would be simply to raise the contributions to the 'community chest.' If it is apparently not so 'easy,' let us address ourselves first to measures which might make it so. The real annual aid transfer (the untied grant equivalent) is at present probably only something like 3 billion US dollars, at most, by the time you discount official data in the various necessary ways. The World Bank has said that the absorptive capacity is much larger than the aid funds that are at present being offered and I am prepared to take their word for it. But even if it were not, the absorptive capacity for social investment, sewers, and that sort of thing, and the absorptive capacity for consumption is surely fairly close to infinite.

Now that so many econometric studies seem to be showing that capital, sheer capital, is not all that important in the global development process, perhaps the emphasis I am giving to resource flows may seem inappropriate. I do not really think so. There is, however, another area which I think merits a great deal more attention. This has to do with stimulation of technical change or productivity growth, which, according to the evidence, apparently *is* causing growth and which I believe is or could be stimulated through increased aid effort. The determinants of technical change are not clearly established, but we know enough to be aware that research activities, sheer knowledge, and advance in the field of education has had a great deal to do with it. The most dramatic breakthrough in the development front in the last few years has been the development of new varieties of seeds (maize, rice and wheat), and this development was achieved with very small inputs. It was achieved by concentrated foundation research efforts. I have no doubt that there are all manner of similar sorts of potentially high yielding but fairly risky investment activities, many of which will have important productivity raising effects, which could and ought to be financed by the World Bank and/or other types of development institutions. It is how to stimulate and finance these sorts of smaller, experimental, risky investments in the research sphere, and how to disseminate the results, which I think is most required. (When such activities are financed, incidentally, I see no reason why they should be financed by loans, IDA loans or any other kinds of loans. IDA loans in any case are 80 to 85 per cent concessionary. You might as well give the money and have done with it.)

There are many other issues in this whole area that I think could be discussed here but let me simply make one last point. Particularly at a time when within the developing world itself there is increased interest in the need for decentralization in decision-making and financial authority, I think there is room for much more thought about the possibility of decentralization of aid administration and, in particular, of World Bank Group activities. More authority for people on the spot, for local offices to distribute funds (perhaps up to stipulated limits) on local projects, local experimental schemes, research activities, and so on without constant reference to the head office except perhaps for larger schemes, could be very productive. This might get a whole lot of potentially high-yielding activities quickly off the ground. Another area in which decentralized decision-making might be useful is in the middle ground between project loans and so-called country programme loans. Aid can surely be granted for some broad purpose within a particular country with much more flexibility available to the recipient than has been customary as to its use. One could, for instance, provide flexible support for efforts relating to a single crop, or, a single area, perhaps to a single sector such a s agriculture. Aid allocations, in which the details of the expenditures are left to the local level, have not received sufficient experimentation.

My overall feeling is that the World Bank Group which is at present, for better or for worse, the only hope for concentrated international attention to the development problem, simply does not have the necessary influence or prestige. I think we could devote a great deal more attention and thought to ways in which we might develop this group so that by 1985-90 we are closer to a first-best sort of world with a strong multilateral aid distributing body with branches around the world empowered to make quick flexible responses to immediate research and investment possibilities. While on the way to this objective, by all means let us continue to tinker with all these interesting exercises in the fields of supplementary financing, buffer stocks, commodity schemes, preferential access for manufactured products, and many more.

PART 4 ASSESSMENTS

Pierre-Paul Schweitzer

A REPORT ON THE FUND

Like most revolutions, the movement which culminated at Bretton Woods in July 1944 was the product of its time. Three main considerations motivated the pioneers of that movement. These were, first, a realization that, as a result of the war, the international economy had been violently disrupted; second, a fear that after the war the vicious cycle of boom and slump would be repeated; and, third, a recognition that to cope with these problems much greater international co-operation would be necessary than had prevailed before 1939.

How severely the war was breaking up the established economic relationships became increasingly clear as it went on. By 1944 the signs were unmistakable. Only the United States and Canada among the major trading nations of the prewar world showed promise of emerging with little economic hurt. Continental Europe was a scene of widespread devastation; Japan too was crumbling; and the United Kingdom had spent practically all its reserves and run up massive debts to pay for essential imports. Despite the relief afforded by Lend-Lease, World War II had carried much further the transference of economic power across the Atlantic.

There was a common fear that, as after World War I, a brief boom would be followed by a disastrous slump. By 1920 wholesale prices in most European countries were more than three times as high as they had been in 1913. Within the next two years these prices had fallen by 50 per cent. Not until 1925 had world trade surpassed its prewar level, and only a few precarious years of prosperity supervened before the onset of the Great Depression.

Partly as a result of this disaster, governments in the thirties were beginning to place a high and stable level of employment in the forefront of their policy aims. The first effects of this preoccupation, however, had been to stimulate economic nationalism. Competition for exports had led to chaos in the exchanges, as country after country devalued in the hope of undercutting its neighbours. The paraphernalia of exchange restrictions, multiple rates, and fluctuating currencies proliferated. It may be claimed that these devices served as a support for domestic recovery programmes, but a high price was paid in terms of uncertainty and international disruption.

Little had been done by way of co-operation to repair the fragmentation of the world economy. The most abitious attempt was the Tripartite Agreement in 1936, which was prompted by the devaluation of the French franc and sought to concert among its members safeguards against the effects of any further devaluations. But it had no means of enforcement and no separate organization to give it permanence; and it was of little consequence.

So it was that the countries that came together in 1942 and 1943 to prepare the way for Bretton Woods brought to their discussions a common determination to adopt a code of financial conduct in the international sphere which would outlaw competitive depreciation of exchange rates, a common recognition that international financial assistance would be needed to assist countries to abide by this code, and a readiness to relinquish some part of national authority in the interests of the international community as a whole.

The International Monetary Fund was created as the embodiment of these principles. We may now look back across twenty-five years to appraise the handiwork of its founders and to see what lessons intervening experience holds for the future conduct of international monetary management. If I dwell rather on the weaknesses associated with the system created at Bretton Woods, I do not mean to disparage its achievements, which are recognizably outstanding. The dream of Bretton Woods — or, as many cynics were to say for more than a decade after the conference, the illusion of Bretton Woods — was the unrestricted convertibility for current transactions of at least the major currencies. This became a reality some ten years ago and in many cases was extended also to capital transfers. The real output of the membership of the Fund, their trade in goods and services, and the flow of investment capital among them have expanded beyond all expectations and with barely any interruption. The achievements of the system and of the related revolution in national policies have changed our whole way of describing the economic climate. We talk much less of the business cycle, much more of rates of growth in real income. Insofar as the economies of member countries are still subject to cyclical phenomena, we no longer describe these in the terms used thirty years ago – 'prosperity and depression.' The problems have been transposed to a different key and we speak now of 'overheating' and, occasionally, 'recession.'

Yet in recent years the system has betrayed signs of strain in a notorious series of currency crises. Less spectacular but more ominous have been the introduction in some cases of restrictions on current transactions, the tinkering with border taxes, the reimposition or tightening of capital controls, and the sluggish growth of aid. These developments have given rise to a keen debate on the adequacy of the system established a generation ago. As I said, I propose to concentrate on those aspects of the system where performance has been less satisfactory. In that context, I shall deal first with exchange rates, second with the adjustment process, and third with the provision of adequate reserves.

The current controversy has centred chiefly on the exchange rate regime. It has been seriously questioned whether the par value system and its limited freedom for market rates to move on either side of parity is not unduly rigid and outmoded in the present world. This system was intended to provide a stable environment which, by encouraging commercial interchange, would stimulate the growth and sharpen the efficiency of the world economy and its constituent parts. Stability, as the Fund has stressed in the past, does not mean rigidity. Specific provision was written into the Articles of Agreement for changes in par values; and where countries – in deficit or surplus – can no longer maintain broad equilibrium over time in their external payments without having to incur undue unemployment or price inflation, it is wholly proper that this provision should be used.

Yet in some instances, despite the existence of this provision, exchange rates that ceased to be appropriate were maintained too long. And this has contributed to the persistence of payments disequilibria, the encouragement of speculation, and crises in the exchange markets. Moreover, the rigidity of exchange rates in this sense has sometimes led to corrective measures of a kind that deny the very purposes which the par value system seeks to promote.

It is also true that the present framework differs in at least one important aspect from the world envisaged when the Articles of the Fund were agreed. The drafters were well aware that a country might have to alter its exchange rate in response to relative changes in its real economic position. But they did not envisage that a country would have to be so much concerned about the public's changing views on the strength of its currency. Speculative capital movements were to be suppressed rather than financed; indeed, limitations were put on members' access to the Fund to finance capital outflows. While the liberalization of payments for capital transactions has been a major factor in bringing about an integrated world economy, it has also greatly increased the possibility of sudden pressures on exchange rates, notably when underlying economic developments give reason to suppose that an adjustment would be appropriate. In their efforts to minimize speculative capital movements, moreover, countries have frequently felt obliged to make firm pronouncements on the fixity of their exchange rates, and this has inevitably made it more difficult for policy to respond to changed economic conditions.

The strains thus experienced by the system have led to suggestions that it might function better if there were more room for exchange rates to change. Various possibilities have been advocated for various kinds of flexibility intended either to facilitate adjustment in the basic balance of payments or to provide more incentive for equilibrating speculation or to combine these two objectives in some degree.

These suggestions deserve careful study in the full context of the achievements of the present system, of its weaknesses to be sure, but also of the grave disturbances of which the drafters at Bretton Woods still had the most immediate and vivid recollections. It is true that the world's financial system has been badly rocked in the last few years; and it would be foolish to minimize these disturbances. But it is also true that they have been overwhelmingly financial, not economic, in kind.

It seems to me that the essential characteristics of the par value system remain valid now as they were twenty-five years ago. Stability of exchange rates has made a key contribution to the balanced expansion of the world economy. The major advance toward international co-operation in the economic field that was achieved at Bretton Woods was that the rate of exchange for each currency was made a matter of international concern. It is only by bringing exchange rates under international jurisdiction that the risk of competitive depreciation and other forms of currency warfare can be avoided. It is true that since the end of the war this risk has not manifested itself as a serious one; but this experience at least partly reflects the success of the Bretton Woods system and in no wise justifies dismantling the protection provided by the Articles of the Fund.

In this connection I should like to make one very general point. Governments have in the postwar period increasingly accepted responsibility for the performance of their national economies in terms of employment, output, price stability, and other major economic variables. The rate of exchange has a major impact on all these aspects and is bound to be politically sensitive. In my view, it is therefore unrealistic to suppose that governments would be prepared to accept alternative regimes that would put the rate of exchange at the mercy of market forces alone. Almost certainly rates would continue to be managed and common rules would have to be agreed to forestall any possibility of a reversion to anarchic practices. It is at least open to doubt, however, whether generally acceptable criteria could be worked out in this area.

I believe that any case for change must be convincingly made in light of the interrelated aims – growth and stability – which any system should serve. Beyond this I have no wish to prejudge the outcome of the various studies that are being made on this matter. Nor do I wish to predict whether in the end any changes that might be found desirable would involve primarily some loosening of the provisions of the Articles or a somewhat readier use of the possibilities for par value changes that the Articles contain. In this last respect there might be advantages in members proposing changes in parities whenever there was substantial evidence of fundamental disequilibrium and without necessarily waiting until such evidence was overwhelming.

Although I have so far dwelt almost exclusively on exchange rates, it would of course be wrong to consider this matter in isolation. Changes in exchange rates are one element in the broader mechanism that has come to be called the adjustment process. In certain circumstances rate changes are an indispensable condition for the correction of economic maladjustment, but even so they are part only of what must be a concerted attack on that problem.

The Fund is very much concerned with the adjustment process, as Article I makes plain. One of the purposes of the Fund, in accordance with its other objectives, is ' ... to shorten the duration and lessen the degree of disequilibrium in the international balances of payments of members.' It is inevitable that countries should from time to time develop deficits or surpluses in their external payments; and it is important for the member concerned and, in the case of the main trading countries, for the system as a whole that these should be contained and corrected within a reasonable period of time and in a manner consistent with the other objectives of the Fund. Unfortunately, members' imbalances have not always been notable for the brevity of their duration or the modesty of their size. The long-standing deficits of the United States and the United Kingdom and the surpluses of some continental European nations are serious cases in point.

Against this background some commentators have argued that the international community should formulate and adopt uniform rules for financial policy to introduce an element of automaticity into the adjustment process. That approach tends to underrate the complexities of this world. In seeking to achieve simultaneously a variety of economic objectives of differing degrees of compatibility, countries need leeway to apply that combination of policies which is best calculated to overcome their particular difficulties and takes account also of the range of instruments at their disposal. A mechanistic formula, even if it were operationally feasible or politically acceptable, would inhibit this flexibility of response. At the same time there can be no question that, in the pursuit of their domestic objectives, countries should give adequate weight to the evolution of their external payments. This means that countries should be prepared to co-ordinate and temper their economic policies in light of the implications that these have for other countries and the world economy.

The responsibilities of surplus and deficit countries in the adjustment process have been extensively discussed in the Fund and in Working Party 3 of the OECD. This interchange has been fruitful in identifying problems of common concern and in increasing understanding as to appropriate responses. Having said this, I am bound to add that there remains a gap between understanding and practice. This stems partly from imperfections in economic diagnosis and forecasting. At the same time the tools for implementing policy are often cumbersome to use and lacking in precision when applied.

Yet, after due allowance is made for such difficulties, there remains a basic problem which is political in nature and which has not infrequently impeded prompt and appropriate action. It consists broadly in a reluctance to dampen down excessive aggregate demand until the inflationary process has caused substantial damage; and also in an unwillingness to make necessary adjustments in exchange rates not simply for reasons of national prestige but also because this is no easy option in terms of its effect on the real income of particular sectors of the community. It is not readily apparent to me how this problem, in light of its nature, can be resolved simply by changing the monetary system. To the extent that political will is engaged, it seems necessary that countries should accept that timely action is in their own self-interest in all but the very shortest term. It may be that this is being, or will become, more widely recognized as a result of experience over the last several years. If the chaos of the thirties could be followed by the incomparably more responsible approach of the postwar period, I am inclined to believe that the improvement can be carried further.

It is possible to take encouragement from the fact that countries have made and are making the effort to adjust. The two major deficit countries of past years, the United States and the United Kingdom, have shown much determination in this respect. To improve the severe imbalance in the system, however, persistent action on their part will be necessary for some long while ahead. At the same time the policy reactions of a wide range of other countries will be hardly less important. As the United States and the United Kingdom move into surplus, the payments positions of many other countries will become less easy. This expectation has been confirmed by developments in the first quarter of 1969. During this period the United States, although in record deficit on the liquidity basis, had a large surplus on official settlements account; and the United Kingdom also was running a moderate overall surplus. This situation had an immediate impact on the payments and reserve positions of a number of industrial countries and began to provoke certain defensive reactions.

These recent developments underline an essential requirement of the international monetary system which, though understood by some at Bretton Woods, was not provided for in the structure that emerged. This is the need for a continuing accrual over the longer run of global reserves in a quantity sufficient to permit countries that conduct their international transactions in a responsible fashion to increase their reserves adequately as those transactions expand.

This need was satisfied in the earlier years of the system created at Bretton Woods, although it would perhaps be too generous to say that its architects had clearly foreseen how this aspect would work. The increase in reserves during the fifties and the early sixties was not statistically very large. The annual rate of growth was about 2½ per cent, against an increase of trade in the order of 6 or 7 per cent a year. The main explanation for the fact that reserve growth was nevertheless adequate is found in the massive redistribution of reserves that took place during the period. The United States, especially, and a number of developing countries, that had ended the war with very large accumulated reserves could well afford an absolute decline in their stock. The small amount held by foreign countries in the form of claims on the United States could readily be expanded without hesitation on the part of debtor or creditor. These adjustments together with accruals of newly mined gold permitted the combined reserves of countries outside the United States to grow roughly in proportion to the expansion of their trade. In these circumstances countries were able to sustain that rapid expansion, to liberalize current and — in many cases — capital transactions, and to devote resources to assisting developing countries.

This process of reserve growth ceased to function in about 1965. Such reserve growth as there has been in the past several years has been in the form of monetized credits to countries in balance-of-payments deficit. It is clear that this is no basis for the long-run growth of world reserves.

Fortunately the imagination which twenty-five years ago produced the Articles of Agreement of the Fund has not been wanting in recent years. The proposed Amendment to the Articles provides a constructive solution to the need for deliberate reserve creation that is now materializing as the traditional process ceases to function. The discussions and negotiations that preceded agreement on the Special Drawing Rights facility were protracted and by no means easy. Nevertheless, I think that we can take some satisfaction in the fact that a procedure has been worked out and will soon be available to meet an emerging defect of the system, without the world economy having had to provide the proof, through large-scale misery and dislocation, that adequate reserves are the required lubricant of that system.

It would be strange if we were not deeply concerned about the international monetary scene at a time when financial crises seem almost to have become a regular feature. But it is possible to be too discouraged. A rational means of injecting liquidity into the system has been agreed; and this was a striking instance of co-operation which has been evident, though in widely differing degrees, in other areas. Countries have made the effort to adjust, even if action has too often been tardy. There is certainly need for a less defensive attitude toward exchange rate changes. Beyond that, there remains the basic need for countries to put more emphasis on financial stability in recognition of the economic benefits that this confers. Without that policy disposition, experience will be unhappy under no matter what system. Paradoxically, the very difficulties of these latter years, which have mercifully been still financial in character, may have served to make this increasingly understood.

Harry G. Johnson

A GENERAL COMMENTARY

The two institutions discussed in the preceeding papers really stand at quite different points in their evolution. The IMF stands on the threshold of a major change – as Mr Bernstein put it in his paper, a change probably more important than the foundation of the IMF itself – the change to deliberate, internationalized creation of international reserves on a credit basis. That transition is in hand, but there remain important outstanding questions about how the international monetary system will in fact evolve. The World Bank, in contrast, has pretty well completed the transition from commercial project lender to economic development assistance institution; and the main concern about it is to ensure that it has adequate funds to support this role, the transition having coincided with a marked decline in the willingness of the developed countries to provide aid to the underdeveloped.

There is also the fact that these two institutions raise quite different problems from the viewpoint of professional economists interested in international economic relations. One can distinguish between problems that are intellectually interesting, in the sense that they lend themselves to the application and elaboration of fundamental economic theory, and problems that are socially interesting, in the sense that we are concerned about them through a sense of responsibility to the world in which we live. Most of those present who are interested in the World Bank, I judge, are interested because they are concerned to improve the provisions for assisting the development of the less-developed countries. That is mostly a question of persuading the developed countries to put up far more money; the details of what is done with the money are in large part matters of political and institutional organization about which the economist as an economist does not have much to say. The aspects of the development problem about which he does have something to say involve detailed microeconomic analysis directed at highly specific problems. The Fund, however, raises broad and fundamental questions in monetary theory and macroeconomics with which most economists are at least vaguely familiar, or at least on which they can bring their previous knowledge of these subjects to bear. In the field of development assistance there is much less scope than in the field of international monetary organization for useful discussion of broad principles in which most generally qualified economists can participate.

The Bretton Woods planners really intended to have three institutions, including specifically an International Trade Organization as well as the two we have discussed. The proposal for an International Trade Organization proved abortive, and its place was in fact taken by the General Agreement on Tariffs and Trade. But still the concept was there; whether present institutional arrangements, under which money and development are dealt with in one fairly closely-knit institutional framework based on Washington and trade in a quite separate one based on Geneva, are really the most fruitful either from the point of view of the world economy or of its effects on academic specialization are further issues which ought to be considered.

For example, the question of trade barriers and their impact on development might be raised. Trade barriers do not fall within the sphere of the Fund and the Bank; they fall in the sphere of GATT. Yet in both the development area and the monetary area, what has been going on in trade policy in the past twenty-five years has had important ramifications. Trade liberalization through the two exceptions to the general GATT principle of non-discrimination, customs unions (the European Common Market), and free trade areas (the European Free Trade Association) has meant substantial discrimination against the exports of the less-developed countries; it has also had important monetary implications through its effects in drawing American direct investment to Europe, through stimulating the development of the Euro-dollar market, and through discriminating against American exports, all of which have fed problems back into the international monetary system.

Ronald McKinnon has rightly pointed out that the trade policies of the developing countries themselves are probably a more important obstacle to their development and integration in a growing world economy than the shortage of external finance for development. But the terms of reference of this conference provide no real opportunity to discuss this issue, since neither of the institutions under discussion is concerned with trade policy.

I think the first papers were extremely interesting and useful, particularly to the majority who were not old enough to be aware of or appreciate what was going on at Bretton Woods, let alone be present there or follow the proceedings from outside. They revealed something that surprised me, though I suppose I should have known about it, the importance of Keynes' conversion to liberalism. He was not the most influential British representative present; he was fighting all the time against others who were taking a restrictionist, protectionist view of how the world should be structured in Britain's interest, and he had to fight very hard to make his point. There were other interesting revelations, some of which were surprising by their farsightedness and others by their shortsightedness.

One of the important points that emerged in all sessions is the great difference between the assumptions made at that time about the nature and prevalence, and the possibility of controlling, capital movements and the reality that has evolved since. The capital movements that the system has had to contend with in recent years have not been the 'hot money' movements of the 1930s, but a quite different species made possible by convertibility of currencies, international financial integration, and a vast improvement in the rapidity of international communication. In theoretical terms, the difference is between the speculative and the precautionary motives for holding international money.

Another important point is that the Bretton Woods institutions were designed with a quite different view of the policies required by their existence than now prevails. The World Bank was intended to patch up a defective international capital market, but otherwise to function as a free enterprise type of institution. Instead there has been a vogue for economic planning and an emphasis on the provision of capital on concessionary terms, which has meant a quite different role for the Bank than was envisaged then. In a sense, this is a cycle through which efforts to improve the regional distribution of income within an individual country also passes: intervention starts with the assumption that the remedy is merely a matter of channelling in money which the imperfection of the capital market prevents it from providing, and ends by recognizing a whole complex of educational, social, and institutional problems requiring a major social transformation.

The second group of papers dealt with the actual operations and evolution of the two institutions over the past twenty-five years. Bernstein started from the proposition that the real test of the IMF is not that it has survived and still exists, because these institutions once established invariably find and assert some role for themselves — they have too many high-priced people working for them not to find something useful to do. Instead, he sets himself the test of how good the IMF's thinking has been at various points in the evolving economic history of the period. Robert Mundell and others, in discussing and criticizing the paper, suggested a rather tougher standard – not how good the Fund's thinking has been, but how much leadership it has exercised. (This calls to mind the standard distinction between the politician who leads the people in the direction in which they seem anyway to be set on going, and the statesman who considers the direction in which they ought to be going and persuades them to move in that direction.) Bernstein certainly makes no bones about the IMF having failed at crucial points to take a lead when it could have been taken. The one that he dwells on most was the failure of the Fund to realize that the question of the need for deliberate reserve creation was going to come up, and the consequent necessity for the academic economists (most notably Robert Triffin) to use their independent positions to preach the existence and seriousness of the problem and the urgency of finding a solution for it. I believe that in a finer analysis one could find a number of other directions in which the thinking of the IMF consisted either of denying that a problem existed or of meekly following policy lines laid down by that other eminent Washington institution, the United States administration.

Ray Mikesell's paper was far less controversial. He did a very workmanlike job of tracing the evolution of the Bank. He raised the question of whether, if we really want to provide development assistance, we should do it in this quasi-orthodox-financial form of concessionary loans rather than by straight gifts. We already know from practical experience and from UNCTAD studies that the trouble with giving aid in the form of loans is that they are still loans, not gifts. The recipient is unlikely to realize that there is not that much real aid involved, and to over-commit himself, and then find himself in financial difficulties from which he has to be rescued. The donors wind up giving the aid as a gift anyway, but the process involves much unnecessary abrasive irritation and self-deception on both sides.

Mr Schweitzer's statement of the Fund position was understandably somewhat imprecise but did at least strongly suggest the desirability of increased flexibility of exchange rates. This is a more daring suggestion than he may have realized, since Mundell had stated in effect that exchange flexibility is 'out' and fixed rates – rigidly fixed rates – are 'in,' and that from the theoretical point of view at least greater exchange rate flexibility would amount to no significant change.

The contents of Mundell's contribution are probably more familiar to me than to most readers, since while Mundell and I exist to demonstrate that there is no such thing as a Chicago School – because we come out at the opposite ends of several major issues in this field – I have closely followed the development of his line of thought. It strikes me that there are some major weaknesses in his argument, although I confess to enjoy the historical sweep that he brings to discussions of these matters. I think his paper would be improved by drawing the clear distinction between private dollars and official dollars that McKinnon has drawn in his recent International Finance Series essay. What Mundell is talking about is the private demand for dollars: the use of the dollar as an accounting unit, the development of the Euro-dollar, and so forth involve a private move towards the dollar. The trend is important, and I agree with his argument that much of our trouble has been due to the failure of the authorities of other countries to understand it as a powerful evolutionary movement of history, and their resort instead to blind resentment. But their resentment focuses on the official dollars; and it seems to me quite possible, particularly given the nature of the SDRs, that we may be witnessing, not a conversion from the dollar as an international reserve currency to a substitute international credit reserve, but a transitory pause in the extension of the domain of the dollar. A number of events that might occur, such as the end of the war in Viet Nam and the achievement of stability *à la* Bernstein in the American economy, might well make other countries reconsider whether they are really so opposed to letting the dollar become the basic international money. It is the basic international money now, *de facto*; and it rather surprises me that Mundell did not really offer much of an argument as to why it is desirable to replace this natural growth by an artificial new instrument to be created at the Fund. It is true that most of us who have thought about international monetary reform have always had at the backs of our minds the ideal of a world bank and a new basic world money; but it may be that this is a lust for academic perfection which is anti-historical in spirit, and that it would be more natural for the dollar to evolve into the basic international money with the Federal Reserve – an improved Federal Reserve, one would hope – managing it in the interests of the world economy. In that case the world would obtain the stability that Bernstein has stressed, and most of the current objections to the dominance of the dollar would cease to be relevant.

Mr Prebisch's paper was ostensibly in the development area, but really in the monetary area, for his message provided strong support of the 'link' pro-

posal. I was less surprised by this than most, because it so happens that he and
I testified together – in physical company if not in intellectual spirit – before the Reuss Subcommittee on this very proposal. I am not unsympathetic
to Gerald Helleiner's defence of Prebisch's position – that one has to start
thinking of second-best, or possibly even of third-best, solutions if
one has no hope of obtaining a first-best solution. But from any monetary
theoretic viewpoint the idea of the 'link' is nonsense – and Helleiner was
rather careful to compare it with still worse alternatives in the form of commodity money, and he could have found a still worse one yet by comparing it
with the Hart-Kaldor-Tinbergen scheme which UNCTAD initially flirted with
and which would involve actually consuming resources on a substantial scale
in the process of creating money. Advocacy of the 'link' ignores the fact that
we have already taken domestically, and are set to take on an international
scale, the step of creating money by a credit operation that requires no expenditure of real resources. The objection to the 'link' scheme is that, while it
would involve no real resource cost to the world as a whole, it would involve a
cost to the developed countries in the form of a transfer of real resources to
the less developed countries. This transfer is not a necessary part of the me-
chanics of creating new international credit reserves, and it would impose a
cost of creation of new international reserves on the developed countries
which is both unnecessary and undesirable.

Earlier I referred to the unattractive characteristics of SDRs. I had in mind
particularly the low interest rate they will carry, and I have been informed
that this was deliberate, to make them inferior substitutes for dollars. Various pieces of work that Mundell, McKinnon, and others (including myself)
have done on the question of optimal money supply – the problem comes up
in a variety of contexts – lead to the conclusion that interest ought to be paid
on international reserves at a competitive rate, because otherwise countries
will always be under an incentive to hold too few reserves on average, because
it costs them too little to do without them and too much to hold them, and
they will therefore run them down by investing in real resources instead.
Now, the purpose of having adequate reserves is precisely to persuade countries to choose the policy options which involve holding reserves and using
them when necessary, rather than restrictions and other kinds of undesirable
devices, and to enable them to manage their balances of payments while
maintaining a satisfactory level of employment. If in fact reserve-holding is
taxed by making interest on reserves zero or very low, there will be incen-
tives, first not to create enough reserves, and second for those countries

which have a strong demand for real capital to use new reserves to buy capital goods, so that the reserve creation process will on the one hand not improve the international monetary mechanism and on the other hand will become an international transfer arrangement.

In much of the literature on international monetary reform it has been assumed without much thought that adequacy of international reserves can be achieved simply by creating a larger nominal quantity of reserves, without regard to the costs of holding those reserves. This assumption is fallacious, in terms of pure monetary theory, because money-holders have the choice between holding additional money balances and spending them, and if they find their holdings excessive in relation to the cost of holding them, they will attempt to spend them, and in the process adjust the real value of the total of nominal reserves to the desired level through a process of inflation. In the international monetary context, there is a distinct possibility that the creation of additional international reserves, with costs of holding them deliberately adjusted to make them less attractive than dollars, will simply lead to inflation and remedy none of the defects of the present system – the resort to controls and to the maintenance of undesirably high rates of unemployment.

This theoretical point has the implication that McKinnon draws, namely, that countries will have a fairly strong incentive to hold dollars rather than SDRs, which incentive will prevail at least for smaller and poorer countries and may well prevail for the larger ones once recent resentment of American world political power and of American inflation for domestic reasons abates. A further implication concerns the amount of SDRs that can safely be created, if the amount of SDRs is to be consistent with the maintenance of world price stability. It might well turn out, if confidence in the United States and in the United States dollar is restored at the official level, that the safe level of creation and expansion of SDRs is not all that large. This means, in terms of Mundell's argument, that there may be no need or rationale for consolidating dollars, sterling, gold, and SDRs into a new international reserve asset ('intors'), and in terms of Prebisch's paper that the implementation of the 'link' would in fact not do much to increase the real flow of aid to the developing countries – if Prebisch and his allies are sincerely content to let the amount of SDRs created be governed by the requirements of world price stability.

Let me conclude by commenting on some other issues that have arisen. One is the issue of flexible versus fixed exchange rates. Mundell has attacked the argument for greater rate flexibility by going to the long-run pure theory of the subject and pointing out what is quite correct, that if nobody has any money illusion an exchange rate change will have no permanent effect other than to attract people towards the most stable currency — though there will still be a transitional 'real balance' effect to which monetary theorists have been paying increasing attention. But if it were true that for practical purposes there is no money illusion at all and that people are completely rational in real terms, there would be no problem anyway, because everyone would as a matter of self-interest behave in the way that the contemporary proponents of 'income policy' seek to impose on them, and seek wage and price increases no greater than the real economic forces will allow. The real problem is that economic actors seek, and policy allows, monetary gains larger than the real situation allows. It is for this reason that there is on the one hand a case for devaluation as a corrective measure under the present international monetary system, and on the other an argument for a floating exchange rate system as an alternative to the present system. Of course, everyone knows or ought to know that in neither case will the remedy work unless it is combined with appropriate overall policies aimed at keeping control of the relation between productive capacity and absorption.

It is at this point that I must take issue with Sir Roy Harrod, who maintains that economists really do not know anything about the workings of devaluation, that inflation is built into the economic system in a mysterious way, and so forth. I believe on the contrary that economists do know quite a lot about this problem area, but that Sir Roy's views reflect the special circumstances of England, where relevant economic knowledge has been suppressed by the success of the 'Keynesian Revolution' and the dominance of a 'vulgar' version of Keynesianism which abstracts almost completely from the monetary side of a monetary economy — with the almost sole exception of the belief that the monetary authorities can cut down on private spending by denying socially inferior citizens access to bank credit, the inferiority of these citizens guaranteeing their inability to think of an alternative source of financing for their expenditure plans.

In principle it is easy enough to explain the initial failure of the British devaluation of 1967, as reflected in the failure of the current account to improve as expected and the inflationary trend of wages and prices. Even in terms of vulgar Keynesianism, it is clear enough that an improvement in the balance of payments on current account requires a reduction of absorption relative to productive capacity. The British government, having for so long pronounced publicly that devaluation was unthinkable, refused itself to think about it; hence it was extremely slow in reinforcing devaluation by the necessary measures to reduce aggregate demand. Nor, in its approach to reducing aggregate demand, did it utilize readily available developments in macroeconomic and monetary theory; instead it relied on the crude concepts of vulgar Keynesianism.

The basic difference between the Keynesian approach and a modern (quantity-theoretic) approach to such problems is that, as Mundell has mentioned, the Keynesian approach is built on static expectations about prices and interest rates, and also that it rests on the assumption that current consumption expenditure is predominantly determined by current cash income receipts. But in a full-employment economy, such as has approximately been maintained for the past twenty-five year period that we have been discussing, the public does form expectations about the future course of prices – and if it is too stupid itself to do so, the news media will be happy to inform it. Those price expectations will influence both consumer spending behaviour and the level of money interest rates. Consequently, if vulgar Keynesianism expects that higher taxes on current income and expenditure will deter consumer expenditure when the higher taxes are expected to be transitory and prices are expected to rise, and if it interprets an increase in interest rates to historically high levels as restrictive when rapid inflation is expected and the money supply is allowed to expand far more rapidly than is consistent with the feasible rate of growth of real output, it will have only itself to blame for failure to understand why its economic predictions have gone wrong.

One particular aspect of the immediate consequences of devaluation that has puzzled many British economists, but which is easily understandable in terms of absorption and monetary theory, is the apparent paradox of the success of devaluation in increasing exports and its failure to decrease imports. Clearly, if the level of absorption is unchanged, any increase in exports must be exactly matched by an increase in imports, to replace the goods and services that an increase in exports is abstracting from domestic absorption. The failure of the official forecasters to anticipate this possibility is attributable to their reliance on a basically 'elasticity' approach to forecasting, coupled with their concentration on the assumed effectiveness of Keynesian methods of controlling aggregate demand to the exclusion of the influence of expectational and monetary factors.

One particular aspect of this failure – which straddles both United Kingdom and United States experience and calls attention to an institutional point that economists tend to overlook — is that while we theorize about central banks as if their main aim was to give us full employment, price stability, and a variety of other economic goodies, their primary objective in operational terms is to help the government to float its debt on the most favourable possible terms. If, as has been the case in the United Kingdom for some years now, interest rates are being pushed up by inflationary pressure and expectations of both domestic and foreign origin, and monetary policy aims nevertheless at minimizing the cost of placing the public debt, there is a built-in mechanism of automatic monetary expansion which will inevitably spill over into both domestic inflation and balance-of-payments deficits. British policy has belatedly begun to learn this lesson and apply it to policy-making — which is a major reason why devaluation is beginning to appear as a success after all.

Abbreviations

AID	Agency for International Development
CIAP	Inter-American Committee for the Alliance for Progress
DAC	Development Assistance Committee
DLF	Development Loan Fund
ESOSOC	Economic and Social Council
EPU	European Payments Union
G 10	Group of Ten
GAB	General Arrangements to Borrow
GATT	General Agreement on Tariffs and Trade
GNP	Gross National Product
IBRD	International Bank of Reconstruction and Development
IDA	International Development Association
IDB	Inter-American Development Bank
IFC	International Finance Corporation
IMF	International Monetary Fund
ITO	International Trade Organisation
MSA	Mutual Security Administration
OECD	Organisation for Economic Co-operation and Development
OPA	Office of Price Administration
PL 480	Public Law 480 (US Congress)
SDR	Special Drawing Right
SEC	Securities and Exchange Commission
SUNFED	Special United Nations Fund for Economic Development
UNCTAD	United Nations Conference on Trade and Development
WP 3	Working Party 3

Contributors

Edward M. Bernstein, President, EMB Ltd

John J. Deutsch, Principal, Queen's University

Richard N. Gardner, Henry L. Moses Professor of Law and International Organization, Columbia University

Sir Roy Harrod, former Nuffield Reader in International Economics, Oxford University

Gerald K. Helleiner, Associate Professor of Economics, University of Toronto

Harry G. Johnson, Professor of Economics, London School of Economics and University of Chicago

William A. Mackintosh, late Principal, Queen's University

Raymond F. Mikesell, W.E. Miner Professor of Economics, University of Oregon

Robert A. Mundell, Professor of Economics, University of Waterloo

A.F.W. Plumptre, Principal, Scarborough College, University of Toronto

Raul Prebish, former Secretary-General, United Nations Conference on Trade and Development

Louis Rasminsky, Governor, Bank of Canada

Grant L. Reuber, Dean of Arts, University of Western Ontario

Pierre-Paul Schweitzer, Managing Director, International Monetary Fund

David W. Slater, President, York University

Robert M. Stern, Professor of Economics, University of Michigan

DATE DUE